# SEVEN SOVEREIGN QUEENS

BOOKS BY

# GEOFFREY TREASE

*The White Nights of St. Petersburg*
*The Red Towers of Granada*
*Seven Stages*
*Follow My Black Plume*
*A Thousand for Sicily*
*Victory at Valmy*
*Escape to King Alfred*
*Message to Hadrian*
*The Seven Queens of England*
*Seven Kings of England*
*The Silken Secret*
*Web of Traitors*
*Cue For Treason*
*Sir Walter Raleigh: Captain and Adventurer*

GEOFFREY TREASE

# Seven Sovereign Queens

THE VANGUARD PRESS, INC.
NEW YORK

# CONTENTS

# ILLUSTRATIONS

## *Half-tones*

## *Maps*

# FOREWORD

The seven rulers whose life-stories are told in this book have been chosen because, like the seven Queens of England in an earlier volume, they were sovereigns, not consorts. That is to say, they wielded power in their own names, even though in some cases they were also the wives of kings or emperors. English sovereigns, like Victoria and Elizabeth I, have not been included, since they were treated in the earlier volume. Otherwise, most of the outstanding women rulers in western history have found a place in this gallery, though some readers may wonder at the omission of Mary Queen of Scots and Elizabeth of Russia. Mary, the author felt, has been more than adequately dealt with by countless other writers, and Elizabeth appears prominently in the chapter devoted to her successor, Catherine the Great. If seven is to remain seven, and not become eight or nine, an author must make the best decision he can, and stick to it. As for Boudicca, or Boadicea as she used to be called, it is true that she does not equal the other queens either in historical importance or in the amount known about her, but she has become such a legendary character that it is worth while to disentangle the fact from the fiction. Also, though misty as a character, she earns her place by illustrating the high noon of the Roman Empire, between its dawn in Cleopatra's time and its twilight in Placidia's.

# I . Cleopatra, 'Lass Unparalleled'

One of her earliest childhood memories must have been the Pharos, the slender wand of glistening white marble soaring almost six hundred feet into the blue Egyptian sky. Strangely, when dark fell, its tip flowered with fire, flickering red among the cold stars. It was to warn sailors, she was told, and point the way into the Great Harbour. The coast was low and flat, treacherous with rocks and shoals. Without a lighthouse it would have been hard to steer a true course for Alexandria.

Alexandria, where the Princess Cleopatra was born sixty-nine years before Christ, was no more Egyptian than she was.

It looked, felt and sounded like a Greek city. Alexander the Great had planted it there in 332 B.C. on a strip of land with the Mediterranean in front and the Lake of Mareotis behind, shimmering with papyrus reeds. When he died in 323 B.C., and his generals divided the empire he had won, Ptolemy had taken Egypt and made himself a king, with the new port as his capital.

For well over two hundred years his descendants had ruled there. Ever richer and more beautiful, Alexandria became a city of well-planned streets and splendid waterfront palaces, with a theatre where the plays were Greek, a library where the books were Greek and a sports centre where athletes trained for the Olympic Games. Alexandria looked seawards to Europe, not inwards to the African desert.

Cleopatra had not a drop of Egyptian blood. She was pure Macedonian Greek, with straight nose and fine eyes, wide-spaced under delicately drawn eyebrows. Plutarch, writing a century afterwards, suggests that 'her beauty was not in itself altogether incomparable nor such as to strike those who saw her'. It was rather her charm and vitality that conquered men.

She grew up in her father's palace, which stood amid gardens adjoining the Temple of Isis, on a spit of land between the Great Harbour and the open sea.

Her father was Ptolemy XIII, a feeble king nicknamed Auletes, 'the Flute-player', because when he was not too drunk he performed on that instrument quite skilfully. It was the only thing he did well. Most of the Ptolemies had a nickname because their official names were so seldom varied: nearly all the boys were called Ptolemy and many of the girls Cleopatra, the famous one being the seventh. The name meant 'having a renowned father', which in her case was unintentionally ironical. The name of her mother, the Flute-player's second wife, is not on record.

Cleopatra had two younger brothers, both called Ptolemy, and a sister Arsinoë. She had also two elder half-sisters, Cleopatra and Berenice, born of her father's previous marriage to yet another Cleopatra. To make matters still more confusing, the Flute-player's first wife had also been his sister, a point that needs explaining.

Marriages between brother and sister, though forbidden by religion or custom in most parts of the world, were an ancient royal tradition in Egypt. The original reason was that the kingdom was legally inherited by a Pharaoh's eldest daughter, not his son. As he usually wanted his son to succeed him, the simplest solution was for the son to marry the daughter. The Ptolemies, aware that they were Greeks and outsiders, had found it a custom worth continuing. So, over two centuries, there had been a good deal of inbreeding, with resulting degeneracy of the family, although now and again there had been a healthy infusion of fresh blood through marriage outside their kin, as in the case of Cleopatra's mother.

It was an odd family to be born into. When not marrying, they were murdering one another. Half the Ptolemies had been guilty of this. The earlier Cleopatras had an equally frightful record. The future queen grew up in a palace that was outwardly bright and festive but, to those with long memories, dark with dried bloodstains. With a knowledge of Cleopatra's family history it is easier to understand her behaviour in later years.

Otherwise, nothing is known of her childhood. It is uncertain how old she was when her mother died.

At this date the Romans had spread their power almost completely round the Mediterranean. Egypt and a few other lands in North Africa and Asia Minor remained free in name, but none dared to quarrel with Rome. Her legions were all-conquering. Her galleys ruled the waves.

There was not yet an emperor. Rome was still a republic ruled by a senate and elected ministers. But by the time Cleopatra was old enough to take an interest in foreign politics, Rome was drifting towards dictatorship, with two or three strong men competing for supreme power. One was Pompey, whose friendship her father tried to win with a large gift of money. Another, less known in Egypt, was Julius Caesar.

When Cleopatra was ten, Ptolemy paid a state visit to Rome, distributing lavish bribes among the senators and other useful people. It was well he did so. No sooner had he arrived home than the citizens of Alexandria rose in revolt, drove him out, and set his daughter Berenice on the throne. The Flute-player returned to Rome as a refugee. Berenice strengthened her position by marrying a man of great ambition and ability, Archelaus, who was also well thought of by Pompey.

For the next few years Cleopatra did not see her father. He was busy in Rome, plotting to regain his kingdom. Berenice and Archelaus reigned unchallenged in Alexandria.

How did Cleopatra get on with them? What did she feel about her father? There is no record. But she was no fool, and she was old enough now to take an interest in state affairs, especially since in Egypt they were usually mixed up with family quarrels. Her second half-sister died, making her the next in line of inheritance, a perilous position in itself. It would have been quite in keeping with tradition if Berenice and her husband had removed their possible rival.

Whatever fears haunted her girlhood, Cleopatra grew up with a keen sense of fun that sometimes showed itself, even in later life, in practical jokes and high-spirited foolery. Shakespeare's phrase, 'a lass unparalleled', rings oddly if she is pictured as a statuesque figure of tragedy. Yet if the facts are studied, 'lass' fits one side of her complex personality. She *could* rise majestically to the great occasion. She could also knock on doors like any small boy, and run giggling away.

She had a gift for foreign languages. A cultured person then needed Greek, with Latin if possible, but the Ptolemies had seldom troubled to master Oriental tongues. Cleopatra, however, became famous for being able to talk fluently with men of many nationalities.

Alexandria had gradually replaced Athens as the main centre of Greek scholarship and science. So, all her life, Cleopatra mixed with artists and intellectuals. How much

4

she really shared their interests it is hard to say, but she gave them support and encouragement. It was she who brought to Alexandria the King of Pergamum's superb library, two hundred thousand manuscripts.

When she was fourteen, the Flute-player's schemes bore fruit. Moving from Rome to Asia Minor, and promising an immense bribe of ten thousand talents (equivalent to perhaps ten million dollars or several million pounds sterling today), he arranged for the Roman army in Syria to march across the Sinai desert and the Nile delta to restore him to his throne.

The Alexandrians had no desire to fight Roman legions. The palace guards mutinied, killed Archelaus, and opened the gates. At the head of the Roman cavalry rode a muscular, curly-headed young giant, Marcus Antonius. It was then that Cleopatra had her first glimpse of the man who, as 'Mark Antony', was to be linked with her in history and legend.


Little seems to have resulted from this first encounter, though Antony stayed some time in Alexandria. The Roman forces were not kept there out of kindness to Ptolemy, who now scuttled back to his palace and celebrated by having Berenice put to death. The Romans remained simply to make sure of their money. They took over the tax-collecting. It was clearer than ever that Egypt was becoming a mere satellite state.

In one of his soberer moments Ptolemy laid aside his flute and drew up his will. He sent a copy to be filed in Rome. He left his kingdom jointly to his eldest daughter, Cleopatra, and his eldest son. It was implied that they would marry, according to Egyptian royal custom. He called upon the Roman Senate and People (the official phrase describing the republic) to act as trustees of this arrangement.

Soon afterwards, Ptolemy died. It was 51 B.C. Caesar had just made his two brief raids on Britain and was still in Gaul, building up his resources to fight Pompey for the supreme power in Rome. Cleopatra was eighteen. Her brother, now King Ptolemy XIV, was only ten. It was therefore easy to postpone the question of their marriage.

The next three years passed uneventfully. For the time being Cleopatra was really the sole ruler of Egypt, but, though her brother was too young to assert himself, she had to reckon with three unscrupulous men who controlled him, his Greek tutor, Theodotos, an Egyptian officer, Achillas, commanding the palace guards, and a eunuch named Potheinos.

This trio could do much as they liked with the boy Ptolemy, but Cleopatra was not to be managed so easily. They therefore schemed to play King against Queen. That was easy. Family affection was not a marked characteristic of the Ptolemies. Cleopatra disliked her younger sister, Arsinoë, and she had even more reason to quarrel with the boy who shared her throne and would some day become her unwanted husband.

Family differences among the Ptolemies were apt to develop, all too literally, into a matter of life and death. Cleopatra saw that for the moment she could not overcome the men allied against her, especially as Achillas had the soldiers on his side. Suddenly it was proclaimed that her brother would be sole ruler of Egypt. Cleopatra fled. She had lost her share of the kingdom. If she lingered, she would lose her life as well.

She escaped to Syria and gathered an army with which to recover her rights. Soon the two forces were glaring at each other near the desert fortress of Pelusium on the Egyptian border, Ptolemy with his three advisers, Cleopatra

6

with her own trusted friends, notably a Sicilian named Apollodorus.

The expected battle never took place.

At this moment the affairs of Egypt were caught up in the greater affairs of Rome, and the Ptolemies' little civil war was overshadowed by another, far more important.

Julius Caesar had brought off his gamble for the dictatorship. He had beaten the armies of Pompey, the only man big enough to oppose him. Pompey, a fugitive but by no means finished, made for Egypt. Remembering his old influence with the Ptolemies, he expected to find help there and renew the struggle with Caesar. He arrived off Pelusium in a single galley and sent his greetings to the King.

This threw the boy's advisers into a fever of doubt. Crafty, calculating men, they had to decide quickly which of the Roman rivals to back. Pompey was there, Caesar (about whom they knew much less) was not. Caesar for the moment was winning, but would he go on winning? They decided there was just one way of ensuring that they would be friends with the man who eventually came out on top: they invited Pompey ashore, and, as he was about to step on to the beach, they had him stabbed to death and his head cut off.

Meanwhile, Caesar was closer than they realized. With a small force he was in hot pursuit of Pompey. Whatever his faults, Caesar was a man of immense personal courage and audacity. To settle once for all with his rival, he was prepared to risk his own life by following him into a probably hostile country.

Unaware of events at Pelusium, he made for Alexandria. Finding neither King nor Queen in residence, he moored his galleys in front of the palace, landed his little army of four thousand men, and installed himself in the guest-rooms. The Alexandrians objected noisily. For some days there was rioting in the streets, with Roman soldiers murdered by the mob, but the isolated position of the palace, with water on three sides, gave him security. He had also two possible hostages in Arsinoë and her little brother, the second Ptolemy.

When his arrival was reported at Pelusium, the Greek tutor Theodotos set off post-haste to cover the two hundred miles to Alexandria, to greet the Roman conqueror and present him with Pompey's head. Caesar made no effort to hide his disgust. The lickspittle Greek was shown the door. The rest of his life was miserable and he came to a terrible end, crucified by Brutus in punishment for his part in Pompey's murder.

Caesar gave honourable burial to Pompey's head and ordered his ashes to be sent to his widow. Then he wrote asking Cleopatra and her brother to avoid hostilities and both come back to Alexandria. He himself, representing Rome, would try to settle their disagreements as their father would have wished.

Ptolemy answered the summons with his chief minister, Potheinos. Achillas followed, with more than twenty thousand troops, despite Caesar's efforts to have the move countermanded. As a result the small Roman force found itself bottled up in the peninsula occupied by the palace, outnumbered five or six to one by the Egyptian army holding the rest of the city. At the same time Caesar, however respectful to the boy King who was his host, had really added Ptolemy and Potheinos to his bag.

One vital character was still missing from the stage. Cleopatra could not easily accept Caesar's invitation. If she travelled overland to Alexandria she would put herself at the mercy of Achillas. At sea she could be intercepted by Egyptian galleys. Potheinos would stick at nothing if he could lay hands on her inside the palace.

Of Caesar she was not afraid. If only she could reach him, she felt confident that he would give her justice. She therefore resolved on a plan.

She was twenty-one, petite, a featherweight: only a girl of her small build and spirited nature would have considered such a scheme. She would enter her royal home disguised in a way that would defy recognition by the oldest of the retainers. She would go rolled up in a long cylinder of bedding, with a cord round the middle. Men carrying such bed-rolls on their shoulders were an everyday sight. And who could be trusted to carry this one? Her Sicilian friend, Apollodorus.

The pair of them sailed into Alexandria in a small boat with no companions. Such craft were plentiful at the approaches of the busy port. Apollodorus slipped into the Great Harbour late one October afternoon, and tied up near the palace. Darkness fell, the lights came out along the waterfront, the beacon blazed from the top of the Pharos. He stepped ashore, heaved his burden on to his shoulder, and walked calmly past the Roman sentries.

His luck held—or his ingenuity. Within a few minutes he had reached Caesar's quarters and the presence of the dictator himself. Only then did he set down the bed-roll, untie the cord, and help the ruffled and dusty Cleopatra to her feet.

Caesar had a keen sense of humour as well as an eye for an attractive girl. From that moment the two were friends, and soon they were more than that.

Caesar was now in his early fifties, old enough to be Cleopatra's father but not too old to win a young woman's heart. Indeed, he had been winning hearts and often breaking them from boyhood onwards. He had been married and divorced several times—that was common

9

enough among the Roman upper classes—and his other love-affairs had been innumerable.

He now saw before him a charming, intelligent and good-looking Greek girl, appealing to him for protection. She, in her turn, saw a lean, weather-beaten, still sharply handsome soldier, a man who apart from everything else was a splendid horseman, a graceful swordsman, and a powerful swimmer.

And there was so much else. Caesar was not only one of the greatest men in history, he was also one of the most complicated. Brilliant as a general, he had, it is true, destroyed enough human lives to place him in the category of a modern war criminal—yet his ruthlessness always had a purpose, he had no taste for cruelty, and when he felt he could afford to show mercy he did so. In any case, it is unlikely that Cleopatra knew much of his doings in far-off Gaul. If he was a destroyer, he was also a builder and creator: now that his rival Pompey was out of the way, he was full of constructive schemes and reforms. He was a writer and a thinker, as well as a man of action, a far-sighted dreamer on the grandest scale, who turned the old-fashioned Roman Republic into the Roman Empire, though he did not live to become the first emperor. At the same time he was scandalous in his private life, immoral, a spendthrift, utterly unscrupulous.

He was also—and whatever else Cleopatra failed to realize she was well aware of this—the unchallenged master of the civilized world.

They talked late into the night. In the morning Caesar sent for Ptolemy. As the boy goggled at sight of his sister, whom he had fancied many miles away, Caesar gave him a severe lecture on his disobedience to his father's will and told him to make up the quarrel. Ptolemy rushed from the room, calling out that he had been betrayed and was done for, and peevishly tearing off his royal diadem. This started a mighty hullabaloo as the news spread beyond the palace precincts and a multitude of Achillas's soldiers joined with a mob of Alexandrian citizens to demonstrate outside the gates. Caesar went out and faced them with his usual unruffled air, made a speech, and got them to go away. Then, in the calmer atmosphere of the palace, he persuaded Ptolemy to attend a formal council with his sister, at which he recited the terms of Ptolemy XIII's will and made them agree to rule together again in harmony.

For the next few months Caesar and Cleopatra enjoyed the gay and comfortable life of the court. Both believed in pleasure and both had recently passed through a period of acute strain.

Even now, only a man with Caesar's nerves could have relaxed. Danger was ever-present. An Egyptian fleet lay in the harbour, an Egyptian army stood at the palace gates, there were spies and plotters on every side. No one believed that the agreement with Ptolemy would last.

Cunningly Potheinos worked to turn the tables. He spread stories that Caesar was robbing the King of his treasure. He had the golden vessels in the temples melted down and the King's meals served on cheap earthenware. With propaganda gestures like these he stirred up the citizens, and at the same time he corresponded secretly with his confederate, Achillas, outside.

There was Arsinoë, too. She was opposed to Cleopatra and this Roman intruder, but she had little more use for her brother. If he would not escape, she would. So Arsinoë got away, with her own chamberlain, Ganymedes, and joined Achillas at his headquarters. But it was soon clear that they did not see eye to eye with him, for Ganymedes was encouraging the princess to seek power herself, whereas Achillas remained loyal to Ptolemy.

Caesar and Cleopatra had a fair idea of these intrigues. Caesar's barber had a specially good nose for gossip. It was he who brought Caesar definite evidence: Potheinos was becoming desperate to escape from the palace with the King, so that they could join up with Achillas and scotch Arsinoë's scheme, and to achieve this he was planning to murder Caesar. This was more than Caesar's easy temper could stand. He had Potheinos arrested and immediately beheaded. Shortly afterwards he heard that Ganymedes had murdered Achillas, and taken over his role as the most dangerous Egyptian leader at liberty.

Caesar had long ago sent for reinforcements, but they took time to arrive. In the meantime he secured his position on the royal peninsula. He barricaded the land approaches and sent a raiding party across the harbour which burnt most of the Egyptian fleet at its moorings. His worst worry was when the besiegers poisoned his fresh-water supply, which ran underground from the Lake of Mareotis. He led a sortie into the town to stop this, but was forced back by stiff opposition. Luckily he was able to find new supplies of drinking water by digging wells inside the royal perimeter. Cleopatra's worst moment came a little later, when in further fighting in the Great Harbour Caesar's own craft capsized, and he had to swim for his life, struggling out of his scarlet cloak and ducking to avoid the javelins and sling-stones of the enemy.

In due course came news that reinforcements were on the way from Syria, and Caesar knew that he could wind up the affair. He had come to the conclusion that it would be better if Cleopatra were sole Queen of Egypt, uncluttered by her tiresome young brother. He could be ruthless enough to a dangerous adversary, but it was not in his nature to have the youth liquidated according to the family tradition of the Ptolemies. Instead, he contemptuously

let the King go free. The King went, but now most reluctantly, as though he realized that the world outside was
colder and more perilous. He shed tears and begged to stay,
but Caesar made him go.

Caesar knew what he was doing. If Ptolemy stayed,
it would be hard not to let him act as co-ruler with Cleopatra. If he went to the Egyptian army headquarters, he
would displace his more dangerous sister, Arsinoë. And if
his subjects pushed him into open warfare against the
Romans, that would be excellent, because it would free
Rome from all further obligations to him under his father's
will.

It all worked out splendidly—from Caesar's point of view.
The wretched boy (still only fifteen) was pushed into the
command of an army trying to bar the advance of the legions
across the Nile Delta. Caesar slipped out of Alexandria by
sea to join the relieving forces. There was a two-day battle
before the Egyptians were outmanoeuvred and thrown into
panic. Ptolemy jumped into a river-boat with other
fugitives, it sank, and he died ignobly in the Nile mud.

Caesar hastened back to Cleopatra, this time riding
triumphantly through the streets to the landward gates of
the palace. Now he could tell her that she was, without
further serious challenge, Egypt's Queen.


Her brother was dead, her sister was Caesar's prisoner,
only the younger brother remained to reckon with, and he
was only eleven, no serious problem. The Egyptians may
have regarded him now as King Ptolemy XV, and assumed
that when old enough he would marry Cleopatra, but she
had other plans.

She wanted a real husband. Almost from their first
meeting she and Caesar had lived as man and wife. True,

he still had a legal wife in Rome, Calpurnia, but she had borne him no children, and in pagan Rome that would have been accepted as a fair reason for yet another divorce.

Cleopatra, on the other hand, was going to have a child. She announced that the father was the god, Jupiter-Ammon. Far back in the history of the Pharaohs there had been other cases of royal babies credited with divine fathers, and the idea cropped up frequently in Greek and Roman legend. So no one ventured to contradict the Queen, especially as it was known that the gods took on mortal shape for these occasions, and Jupiter-Ammon might well have disguised himself as Julius Caesar.

While awaiting the arrival of this child, Caesar and Cleopatra made a voyage up the Nile. They sailed in the royal barge, a luxurious river-craft built of cedarwood and cypress, brilliantly painted and flashing with gold leaf, and divided into staterooms like a small floating palace. A fleet of four hundred galleys and store-ships escorted them, with several thousand soldiers, Roman legionaries as well as Egyptians, and a countless host of attendants.

Now, for the first time, Cleopatra really saw the vast kingdom that was hers. For several weeks the long flotilla crept upstream. They passed Memphis, the Sphinx and the Pyramids. They went on to Thebes, all the way seeing splendid temples and monuments of a civilization that was already ancient and remote even to them. At Aswan the first of the Nile cataracts made further progress laborious. But they had seen enough. Caesar, for his part, had taken in the full scale and richness of Egypt. His restless mind was reaching out to more and more power. In the Roman Empire he was planning there was a key place for Egypt, for her beautiful young Queen, and for the child she was to bear, especially if it was a son.

It was. No sooner had Cleopatra reached home than the

boy was born, and, besides the formal name of Ptolemy, was called Caesarion.

The dictator could stay no longer in Egypt. Urgent business called him to Rome, and then to Numidia, where he had to squash, bloodily, the resistance of Pompey's old followers. Cleopatra and her baby remained in the palace, until word came to join Caesar in Rome and enjoy his official 'triumph', an elaborate programme of festivities awarded to victorious generals by the vote of the Senate.

Caesar's triumph lasted four days, one for each of his great successes, the first being the conquest of Gaul. Egypt was featured on the second day. The procession included giraffes and other African animals still novel to the Roman public, and replicas of Egyptian wonders such as the Pharos. The disgraced Princess Arsinoë was led in chains with the other prisoners, including her confederate Ganymedes, who was put to death straight afterwards in accordance with the brutal Roman custom. Though Achillas and Potheinos were dead, their memory did not escape ridicule: Cleopatra saw their effigies carried by and jeered at by the spectators.

Caesar established her with her suite in a beautiful villa he owned among the gardens on the western outskirts of the city. He himself continued to live with his legal wife, Calpurnia. It seems likely that his first passionate feeling for Cleopatra had dimmed. He was not a man to be faithful to any one, and in these closing months of his life he was wrapped up in his dreams of world power. He did not ignore Cleopatra—he sent an eminent sculptor Archesilaus to make a statue of her and then created a good deal of gossip by installing it in a new temple of Venus—but he was less interested in her as a woman than as a queen useful in his schemes. Caesarion was now almost more important. The baby's resemblance to Caesar was much commented upon. And Caesarion, besides being an heir for Caesar, would in time inherit the crown of Egypt too. For at this time Cleopatra's younger brother, Ptolemy XV, died—whether through foul play will never now be certain.

Cleopatra could not have been happy, shut away in that villa, however beautiful, on the far side of the Tiber. The Romans hated her because of her influence on their leader, yet she knew that this influence was waning. Caesar was no more the debonair soldier, flirting with danger as well as herself in those first weeks in the blockaded palace. He was turning into a power-drunk despot, impatient of criticism, obsessed with ambition.

She was already planning her return to Egypt when, on March 15, 44 B.C., a terrified messenger brought news that Caesar had been struck down in the Senate House and had died at the foot of Pompey's statue.

What would happen to her now, with her great protector fallen? What, indeed, would happen to the empire Caesar had been bringing to birth?

The questions hung together. While the second was being decided, Cleopatra hurried back to Alexandria with her child. They were safe nowhere. But her own palace, in her own kingdom, was better than the villa in Rome.

Shakespeare's *Julius Caesar* gives a roughly truthful outline of what followed: Mark Antony, Caesar's right-hand man, used his famous eloquence to turn the hesitating people of Rome against Brutus, Cassius and the other assassins; a fresh civil war broke out; Antony, with Caesar's great-nephew, Octavian, and an unimportant politician named Lepidus, took over the government and utterly defeated the opposition at the battle of Philippi; the victorious trio, the 'triumvirs', then divided the Roman territories on a

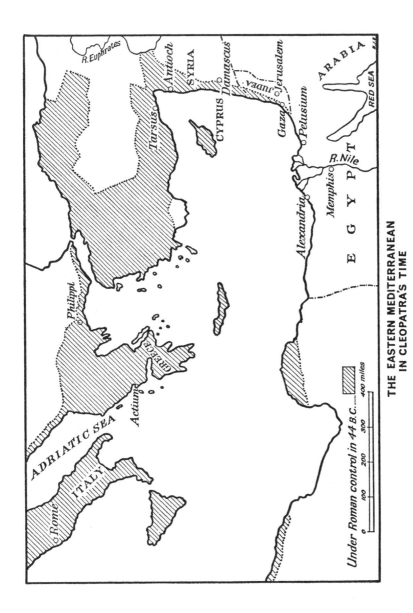

THE EASTERN MEDITERRANEAN
IN CLEOPATRA'S TIME

Under Roman control in 44 B.C. ......

0    100   200   300   400 miles

temporary basis, Antony receiving the richest, the provinces of Asia Minor.

All this took more than three years. Cleopatra stayed quietly in Egypt and Caesarion grew from a baby into a small boy. Had he any chance, she wondered, of achieving the destiny that would have been his if his father had lived? Or was the child in mortal danger? Would he be murdered because he stood in the way of other men's ambitions? Such things had happened all too often in the Ptolemy family, and she had learned by now that these Romans could be equally brutal.

Her reports assured her that there was no love lost among the triumvirs. Lepidus counted for nothing, but there was likely to be a struggle for power between Antony and Octavian. Would either be her friend? Hardly Octavian. He was regarded in Rome as his great-uncle's legal heir. He would never stand down in favour of Caesarion. She would have more chance with Antony. She knew him, she could get on with him, for he had a warm nature, a lusty good humour, a love of life, akin to her own, whereas Octavian had the reputation of being cold, austere and rather priggish. But Antony might have plans of his own in which there would be no part for Caesarion.

She was given a chance to find out when, in 41 B.C., Antony invited her to visit his headquarters at Tarsus, the Cilician city soon afterwards to be the birthplace of St Paul. She accepted without hesitation, took ship, and in due time sailed up the mouth of the Cydnus to where, some miles inland, the river broadened into a placid lake filled with vessels and the city rose white against the green background of the Taurus Mountains.

Antony had often shown his own skill as an actor, but this time Cleopatra outdid him in theatrical effect. She meant to remind him, and the people of Tarsus, that she

18

was a queen, not an applicant for favours. She staged a magnificent arrival. Plutarch's detailed account is closely followed by Shakespeare in words which only a fool would try to improve upon.

> The barge she sat in, like a burnish'd throne,
> Burn'd on the water; the poop was beaten gold;
> Purple the sails, and so perfumed that
> The winds were love-sick with them; the oars were silver;
> Which to the tune of flutes kept stroke, and made
> The water which they beat to follow faster . . .

Antony had intended to receive her graciously in the public square and was enthroned there ready. But Cleopatra stole the scene. She remained aboard. She was not going to Antony, let him come to her. The splendour of the Egyptian party drew the crowds gaping to the water's edge, leaving Antony neglected on his throne. Some statesmen would never have forgiven her, but Antony had generosity and a sense of humour. He sent word, asking her to dinner. She countered with an invitation to dine with her on board her ship. He accepted with a good grace.

The banquet was of calculated magnificence. It would not be true to say that Cleopatra had put all her resources into it. She was far too shrewd for that. She had come to dazzle Antony and his supporters with a display of Egypt's wealth and to convince them that she would be a valuable ally, but she must not confine herself to a single evening's propaganda, she must hold plenty in reserve.

Even so, her welcome took Antony's breath away. The great saloon of her ship was tapestried in gold and purple, the deck underfoot carpeted with flowers. Thirty-six sat down to dinner; lay, rather, for they reclined on cushioned couches in the Roman and Greek manner. The cups and dishes were of gold, inset with gems. When Antony complimented her on all this opulence, she lightly answered that it was nothing: she would be delighted, since it pleased him, if he would accept it all as a trifling souvenir, the furniture, the gold plate, everything. She had come well prepared for such casual-seeming gestures. The following evening she put on an even more lavish show, presenting the guests not only with the goblets they had drunk from but with horses and golden harness, litters and slaves to carry them, and Ethiopian boy torch-bearers.

She stayed about a month in Tarsus. When she left, she felt sure of Antony.

It was not long before he followed her to Egypt, and through the short winter he revelled in the gaieties of a city second only to Rome and even superior in entertainment.

Cleopatra joined in all his amusements. They rode out hunting in the desert, sailed or went fishing. When darkness fell there were banquets and drinking-parties. Actors and musicians, dancers and gymnasts, jugglers and conjurors, appeared before them in constant variety. Sometimes, in sheer high spirits, the two lovers—as they now were—disguised themselves and ventured into the streets alone, knocking on doors and window-shutters and then running off into the night.

Antony had not Caesar's brain and he was altogether a heartier, cruder character. But he was virile and attractive, with the physique of a good-looking boxer, and he was nineteen years younger than Caesar, and anyhow Caesar was dead. Cleopatra wanted Antony, and badly needed him, as her legal husband, sharing her throne. Like Caesar, he had a wife in Rome, his third, but that need be no serious obstacle. It is no use looking for the ideals of Christian marriage forty years before Christ was born.

The romantic interlude was soon cut short. Bad news

20

arrived: Syria was threatened by a Parthian invasion, helped by local princes in revolt. Antony was co-ruler of the Roman dominions and Syria was his responsibility. He had to tear himself away from the delights of Alexandria.

Six months later Cleopatra gave birth to twins. Her new son she named Alexander Helios ('the Sun') and her daughter Cleopatra Selene ('the Moon') but it was to be three years before she set eyes on their father again.

For the second time in her life Cleopatra had to wait patiently at Alexandria, wondering how the future would turn out.

She could have forgiven Antony for not hurrying back to her immediately. She knew the cares of state, understood that he was in a difficult position, facing foreign enemies and rebels on the battlefield, and simultaneously waging an underground struggle with Octavian. Some of the news that reached her, however, was hard to take. No sooner had she heard that Antony's wife, Fulvia, was dead than another message arrived: anxious to patch up his quarrel with Octavian, Antony had married his rival's sister, Octavia. All his promises to Cleopatra lay in ruins.

She did not despair. She knew that she was not just a woman, to be loved and discarded. She was also the Queen of Egypt, in herself a 'great power', with the wealth, fleets and armies of her country in the complete control of her own two delicate hands. So, too, Antony was a 'great power', not just a man. Sometimes they had to behave like the political forces they represented, and do things they would not have chosen to do as individuals. They could not always be racing down the dark alleys of Alexandria, giggling and knocking on doors. Octavia was not a girl whom Antony preferred to Cleopatra. Marrying her was something forced upon him to save his uneasy partnership with Octavian.

As Cleopatra expected, neither partnership nor marriage lasted long. In 37 B.C. Antony came to the conclusion that he could never work in harmony with Octavian. He would stay in his eastern half of the Roman territories, build up his military strength by foreign campaigns, just as Caesar had once done in Gaul, and then, choosing the right excuse, move upon Rome and settle accounts once for all with Octavian, as Caesar again had settled accounts with Pompey. As a first step, Antony sent Octavia home, clearly intending to divorce her later, and invited Cleopatra to join him in Syria at Antioch.

The lovers were now reunited. It seems as though an Egyptian form of marriage was arranged between them, though it would not have been recognized in the Roman courts. New coins were minted, bearing both heads. Antony's name was henceforth officially linked with Cleopatra's, though instead of using the word 'King' (which the Romans disliked) he invented a new title, 'Autocrator', meaning 'absolute ruler'.

Cleopatra put all the resources of Egypt into the alliance. In return, Antony promised that Caesarion, now ten, should be heir to their combined dominions. In the meantime, the ancient glories of Egypt should be restored by the transfer of many lands long lost to the Pharaohs and now controlled by Antony. Cleopatra's own empire was extended to Arabia, the Phoenician coast, the Lebanon, Cyprus, in fact almost all that region of western Asia except Herod's little kingdom of Judaea.

Antony was planning an expedition into Persia, to fight Rome's formidable enemies, the Parthians. Cleopatra went with him. Though one side of her nature enjoyed luxury, another found pleasure in the freedom of camp life and the stimulus of danger. They had marched only a hundred and fifty miles, however, and reached the River Euphrates, when she realized that she was going to have another child. So, with reluctance, she said goodbye to Antony and returned to Alexandria, by way of Damascus, the Sea of Galilee, Jericho, Jerusalem and Gaza. This route took her across Judaea, where King Herod considered having her ambushed in the mountains and murdered. His councillors persuaded him not to. Cleopatra returned safely to her capital and gave birth to a son. He was, according to custom, named Ptolemy.

Antony's expedition was a failure. Roman attempts to conquer the Parthians always were. Antony was lucky to escape with his life, and a remnant of his proud army, after a terrible retreat over the snow-covered mountains. At last he reached the coast of Syria. By that time Cleopatra was able to sail across and rejoin him, and carry him back to her palace to recuperate.

Antony's failure had a lasting effect upon his character. He drank more, to soothe the nagging ache of his shame. He began to go to seed.

Cleopatra did her best to brace him. The romance was over. She saw through him. But like any other wife she had to make the best of him, and steer him skilfully in the right direction. This, she felt, meant giving up vain dreams of conquest in Central Asia and turning to win Rome instead.

In 32 B.C. Antony sent formal notice of divorce to his Roman wife, whom he had not seen for years. This marked a final break with her brother. The Senate formally deprived Antony of all his legal powers (which did not of course make any immediate difference to his actual control of the eastern provinces) and declared war on the Queen of Egypt.

That war was fought on the west coast of Greece, midway between Rome and Alexandria. Octavian shipped his legions across the Adriatic and established himself in a fortified position on the Gulf of Ambracia, a great sheet of landlocked water with only one narrow outlet, at Actium. Antony faced him there, and Cleopatra brought her own fleet to reinforce his. For some time the adversaries watched each other, and there were only minor skirmishes.

Cleopatra herself favoured naval action. Destroy Octavian's fleet, she argued, and his army would be cut off from its Italian bases. Octavian's legions would rot where they were, while she and Antony sailed across to Italy and marched upon an undefended Rome.

Antony's fellow-countrymen warned him that this was dangerous. Cleopatra was detested in Rome. She was the foreign woman whom the public blamed for all the trouble. They would accept Antony as their ruler if he beat Octavian —both men were Romans after all—but they would not have him foisted on them by an Egyptian. Cleopatra should keep her nose out of this quarrel. It would be better if she would return home.

She saw the force of this argument. She had lived in Rome, had no illusions about the feeling against her there. But could Antony beat Octavian without her help?

It seems that at last a compromise was made. The combined navies would engage Octavian's fleet and destroy it. Cleopatra would then at once sail back to Alexandria with her own sixty ships, leaving Antony to claim the full credit without hurting Roman pride.

The long-delayed conflict took place on September 2, 31 B.C. Cleopatra had secretly loaded her treasure-chests and personal baggage under cover of night. Only her own staff and Antony's knew of her plan to return to Egypt.

The opposing fleets each mustered two or three hundred galleys, packed with heavily armed legionaries, archers and slingers. Octavian's vessels were mostly smaller but easier to handle. The tactics were those of a land battle. The two sides would exchange volleys of javelins, arrows and sling-stones at close range, and then, grappling ship to ship, attack with sword and spear. The ships' captains played their part by trying to ram the enemy vessels with their sharp prows and sink them.

Both Roman fleets formed up in three squadrons. Cleopatra's galleys made a fourth in rear. It was a clear, calm morning. Battle was joined at midday and continued all the afternoon in the narrow outlet of the Gulf. Gradually Octavian's smaller craft began to get the best of it. Cleopatra had often shown her iron nerve, but now she gave way to panic. She thought Antony was done for. All she wanted was to get home and prepare some defence for herself and Caesarion against Octavian's revenge. A north wind sprang up. Such a wind would carry her straight to Alexandria. She gave the signal. All the Egyptian galleys that could disengage themselves from the enemy swung out of the battle and hoisted their big sails.

Cleopatra's impulsive mistake was nothing compared with the sheer panic of Antony when he saw her squadron drawing off. He abandoned his flagship, leapt aboard one of his swifter craft with only two companions, and told the captain to follow the Queen. In a short time they overhauled the Egyptian flagship. He climbed aboard. But Cleopatra had retired to her cabin and for several days would not speak to him. He meanwhile sat brooding in the bow of the vessel as they sped southward to Africa. Octavian's victory was complete. The cities of Greece surrendered to him and he started a murderous purge of Antony's supporters.

The final curtain did not fall for almost exactly a year: on August 29, 30 B.C.

Back in Alexandria, Antony and Cleopatra were of little comfort to each other. They had quarrelled hotly in the past. Now their relations were cold and distant. Cleopatra kept up her royal state in the palace, but Antony began an odd hermit-like existence, utterly different from his normal way of life, in a small villa jutting out into another part of the Great Harbour. Most people wondered why he did not commit suicide, the usual way out for a Roman utterly defeated. Antony, however, lived on. And the inevitable day of reckoning with Octavian drew nearer.

Cleopatra had more excuse for hope. Perhaps she could make some deal with Octavian, save something from the wreck. She nevertheless prepared for the worst. She sent Caesarion up-country with a convoy of treasure and instructions to make his way across to the Red Sea, where he could take ship if necessary for India. In the East he could make powerful allies and one day perhaps return victoriously to his inheritance. She herself planned no escape. She would face it out. But, if she lost, she was determined not to be led in chains through the Roman streets as her sister had been years ago. She experimented with various poisons, to discover a painless means of death.

Towards the end of July, Octavian's army appeared at last in front of Alexandria. For a brief hour Antony pulled himself together, became once more the dashing cavalry general Cleopatra had first seen when she was a girl. He led a sortie and inflicted heavy losses on the besiegers. Elated, he challenged Octavian to single combat, but the younger man contemptuously declined. The next day, Antony decided to make a full-scale attack by land and sea. He had scarcely marshalled his forces on the open ground outside the city gates when he saw, with horror, the whole of his cavalry riding across to surrender to Octavian.

Gazing out to sea, he realized that his galleys also were deserting to the enemy.

Antony's followers had seen that the game was up. Now he too accepted the fact. In despair he galloped back into the city and rushed into the palace. Cleopatra had shut herself up, with only her two ladies-in-waiting, Charmian and Iras, in the mausoleum she had prepared as her final resting place, next to the Temple of Isis. Antony concluded that she had already committed suicide. He stabbed himself, but did not die immediately. Still conscious, he was carried to the mausoleum, and there, with Cleopatra's arms around him, he died.

It was not long before Octavian's messengers were hammering on the door. By nightfall the conqueror had entered Alexandria. Cleopatra found herself under house-arrest. The guards had orders to see that she had no chance to commit suicide. Her position was certainly hopeless. She had charmed Caesar and Antony. She could do nothing with the cold Octavian.

She could only cheat him, ensure that he never paraded her as his captive. Closely watched though she was, the guards allowed a man to bring her a basket of figs, in which a small poisonous snake was hidden, an asp, probably a kind of horned viper. She now prepared for death as though it were some splendid ceremony, taking a perfumed bath, having her hair carefully dressed, and putting on her most magnificent robes, with all her jewels and her royal diadem. She wrote a brief letter, asking Octavian to bury her beside Antony. When his officers broke into the mausoleum an hour or two later, they found her dead.

Octavian gave her an honourable funeral. It was the most generous thing he did. All her possessions he seized: the loot of the palace he used to pay his soldiers, melting down gold and silver plate for the purpose; the main booty, her lands and treasure and property of every kind, he reserved for himself. Coaxing messages were sent after Caesarion, who was still hesitating at a Red Sea port, wondering whether to sail for India. He was lured back to Alexandria and put to death. 'It is dangerous,' said Octavian, 'for two Caesars to be in the world together.'

Now he had no rivals. No Roman stood against him and there was no Ptolemy to lead an independent Kingdom of Egypt. A grateful and frightened Senate voted him the title of 'Augustus'. Under that more familiar name he heads the list of Roman emperors.

## THE YEARS BETWEEN 30 B.C.–A.D. 61

The Rome Cleopatra had had to deal with had been an overgrown, outdated republic, shaking to pieces under the blows of civil war. Augustus, once his purge of dangerous enemies was over, brought order and internal peace. The Roman Empire was firmly established. All round the Mediterranean, stretching northwards to the English Channel, the Rhine and the Danube, was one unified super-state, defended by Roman legions, linked by Roman roads, taxed and governed by Roman officials, using Latin as a common language. Over all that region (most of the then civilized world) was a unity that men are today striving painfully to recreate.

In A.D. 43 four legions invaded Britain to bring that outlying island into the system. The Britons had long traded with the mainland, and were anything but painted savages. They were, however, disunited. About a dozen petty rulers headed as many tribes. Their warriors were brave but undisciplined, no match for the well-equipped, well-drilled Romans. So, gradually and methodically, the legions fanned out across what is now England, building fortified camps and roads, creating yet another province.

By the year 61 they were ready to tackle the wild hills of North Wales and the island of Anglesey. This had become a base for those Britons who still held out, inspired by their priests, the Druids. A new Roman governor, Suetonius Paulinus, resolved to wipe out this trouble-centre. Confident that the rest of the country was under control, he led the bulk of his army into this far westerly corner. It was a fatal mistake. It gave Boudicca her chance to win a blood-stained immortality in the annals of Britain.

Boudicca (or 'Boadicea' as she used to be called inaccurately) is not really of great historical importance, but she has always appealed to people's imagination. It is worth while to strip away the romantic legends and find out precisely what is known about her.

At least there is no doubt what she did in the terrible summer of 61.

# 2. Boudicca, Queen of the Iceni

She was a very big woman, wrote the historian Dio Cassius long afterwards. Used to the smaller women of the Mediterranean peoples, the Romans were impressed by the tall, athletic Celts and Teutons of northern Europe. She was 'terrifying in aspect,' he went on, 'with a harsh voice. A great flood of vivid auburn hair stretched to her knees. She wore a big necklace of twisted gold and a multi-coloured tartan dress, with a heavy plaid over it, pinned with a brooch.'

Boudicca was Queen of the Iceni, a British tribe living in that easterly bulge of the island known today as Norfolk. On two sides lay the North Sea. To the west were almost impassable swamps, the Fens that were later to shelter Hereward. Southwards rose the dense forest of Suffolk, with a thin strip of dry chalkland, like a natural causeway, running clear through it to make the one easy route by which traders could come from the outside world.

In this secluded territory the Iceni lived rather like the early Greeks depicted in Homer's poems. They were farmers, breeding cattle, sheep and above all horses, for which they were famous. They grew corn and barley in clearly marked-out fields: aerial photography can still reveal the pattern of these ancient farms. The people lived in thatched huts of timber and plastered mud. Chieftains, such as Boudicca's kindred, had beamed halls probably as fine as the one Odysseus had come home to a thousand years earlier or as Alfred the Great was to feast in long afterwards.

In such a hall Boudicca grew up. She learned to spin and weave. She wore short-sleeved, ankle-length dresses, of mixed bright colours. The men had loose trousers and cloaks of the same tartan-like material. Women and men alike loved ornaments, brooches and pins, bracelets and studded belts of bronze and enamel, gold rings and amber necklaces and gay beads, blue and green, spotted and lined in white. Traders brought some, local craftsmen made others, for the Celtic tribes had men of great artistry, not only blacksmiths and wheelwrights and harnessmakers and armourers, but men who could produce exquisite decorative work in a flowing style quite different from that of the Romans and Greeks. The polished metal mirror in which the young Boudicca studied her face was, in itself, a demonstration of their skill.

That same artistry went into the gaily enamelled shields, the swords and spears, the iron-plated corselets and the helmets with their towering animal-crests that the men equipped themselves with for battle. These British chiefs fought like the Greek and Trojan heroes in the *Iliad*, still using lightweight chariots in the first skirmishes. They sometimes took their enemies' heads as trophies, an unpleasant habit of which Homer would not have approved, though there was barbarity enough at the siege of Troy. Human sacrifice, too, is exceptional in Homer's legends, but less rare among the Britons. Boudicca must have heard of victims slaughtered by the Druids in their sacred groves, whether or not it was a common enough event for her to have seen it with her own eyes when she was young. The Celtic gods were a bloodthirsty set and they were faithfully served by the Druid priesthood. Some of the festivals were no doubt gay and innocent enough, affairs of drinking and dancing round bonfires. Some survive, under altered names, in the modern calendar: days that Boudicca celebrated as Beltane and Samhain are kept still as May Day and Hallowe'en.

In childhood she heard about the world beyond the Iceni boundaries. She heard of the Romans, who ruled beyond the sea. Old men passed on the story of their leader, Caesar, who long ago had come sailing across with his host. Twice he had come. There had been battles, but he had never come within many miles of the Iceni, and soon he had sailed away. The Romans had not troubled Britain again. Only the merchants came and went across the narrow seas, bringing wine and other southern luxuries to trade for oysters, fine hunting dogs, and whatever else the Britons could offer.

The Britain Boudicca knew as a girl was a free country, divided among about a dozen tribes. There were the Silures in South Wales, the Brigantes in the Pennine valleys, the Atrebates in the softer country round the Thames. Each tribe had its own ruler, but one king, Cunobelin, overshadowed the others. In his thirty-year reign he made himself master of all south-eastern Britain. His territory ended where the Iceni lands began.

The High King Cunobelin ('radiant Cymbeline', Shakespeare called him) held his court at Camulodunum, the 'dun' or fortress of Camulos, the god of War. It was a stockaded town of huts, with a defence system of tremendous banks and ditches like those still to be seen in Iron Age forts that survive elsewhere, usually on lonely hill summits. Camulodunum, however, stood in the low Essex countryside on the River Colne, eight miles from the sea. Today it is called Colchester and boasts that it is the oldest town in Britain. It was old when Boudicca was young.

Cunobelin died about A.D. 40. One of his three sons was

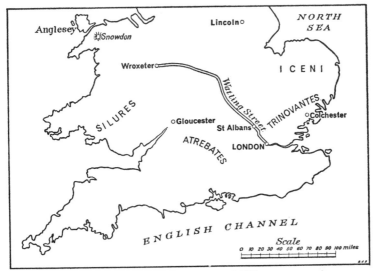

**SOUTHERN BRITAIN DURING THE
ROMAN CONQUEST**

driven into exile and went to Rome. This gave the Romans an excuse to interfere in Britain. The invasion began in A.D. 43. The other two sons of Cunobelin had divided his dominions and led the fight against the legions. One, Togodumnus, was killed. The other, the famous Caratacus, fought on heroically in the western hills, until in 51 he was betrayed to the Romans by Queen Cartimandua of the Brigantes. Long before then—indeed, in the opening campaign—Colchester had been stormed. The Emperor Claudius had travelled there to receive the surrender of eleven British kings. It is said that one came from the distant Orkney Islands. Certainly the Iceni must have been among those who gave up the struggle.

It is not known whether Boudicca was then their queen, or even if she was yet married to King Prasutagus. What is sure, though, is that about seventeen years later she had

33

newly lost her husband and that she had two daughters, probably in their early teens.

Prasutagus had long ago realized the hopelessness of resisting the Romans. Caratacus had done his best, only to end his days as a prisoner in Rome. The King of the Iceni was concerned only to leave his family royally provided for. He did what many another native ruler had done in different parts of the Roman Empire. He made a will, bequeathing half his treasure to the Emperor and the other half to his daughters. The Romans were great believers in law. Surely he could count on the Emperor's seeing that the will was carried out when its terms were so favourable?

Prasutagus did not allow for the Romans on the spot, the tax-collectors and other officials, often unscrupulous adventurers, only out to fill their own pockets. A few years earlier Jesus had bracketed tax-collectors with sinners. Hardly was King Prasutagus buried than these men descended upon his capital like a flock of carrion crows. The chief tax inspector claimed that there was a big loan due for repayment to the imperial treasury. Lands held by the King's relatives were confiscated and their owners made slaves, the common fate of bankrupts under the Roman system. Boudicca protested. Queen though she was, she was scourged in punishment. Order and decency were forgotten, and her young daughters were assaulted.

That was the moment chosen by the Roman Governor of Britain, Suetonius Paulinus, to clean up the resistance of the Druids and their followers on the far side of the country.

Neither Boudicca nor her warriors made the mistake of hasty action. Controlling their fury, they took counsel together and sent out secret messengers to the neighbouring British tribes. While Suetonius mobilized his expedition to North Wales, the plot was hatched behind his back.

The Iceni found their main allies among the Trinovantes of Colchester. These people had plenty of grievances of their own. They had seen their capital taken over by the Romans, first as a garrison town and now as a *colonia* or settlement for veterans. Land had been seized and allotted to ex-legionaries. Colchester was becoming a foreign town. There was a local senate-house, a theatre, all the standard features of a Roman city, paved streets, drains, and such like— amenities the Britons did not appreciate but had to pay for through their taxes. Most unpopular of all was a new temple dedicated to the Emperor Claudius, a most expensive addition and an insult to the religious feelings of the original inhabitants. This, in the town named 'Camulodunum' after Camulos, the War God himself! But what did these Romans care for the sacred beliefs of the Britons? Were they not even now arming to attack the Druids?

So Boudicca found plenty of sympathy with her feelings against the Romans. And plenty of confidence too. If the Britons struck now, when conditions were ideal, they had every chance of liberating their country. The Germans, fifty years before, had wiped out three legions—and the Romans had never tried to conquer them again. What the Germans had done then, the Britons could do now. But it *was* now—or never. They must act while the main forces were in Wales.

Boudicca must have been a woman of outstanding personality or she would hardly have been accepted as leader not only by the Iceni but by the other Britons who joined in the plan. These included, besides the Trinovantes, large numbers from the Midlands and even from more distant tribes in Yorkshire and Dorset.

With the end of winter, she acted. The word went forth. The warriors were to muster. They must not delay to sow their corn: the invaders had ample food-stores and these would soon be captured. When at last the host was assembled, the tawny-haired Queen stepped into her chariot and led them down the road towards Colchester, eighty miles away.

There, the Romans were not unduly worried to hear that the Iceni were on the warpath. They asked London for reinforcements, but London, being a trading centre, could send a mere two hundred soldiers. The commander at Colchester appealed also to Lindum (Lincoln) in the opposite direction. There were plenty of troops at Lincoln, which was the depot of the Ninth Legion, one not employed in the Welsh campaign. Its commanding officer, Petilius Cerealis, started south with two or three thousand men.

Too late Colchester woke to its full danger. The ex-soldiers armed themselves as best they could to swell the thin ranks of the defenders. Suddenly they found that they could not trust the British neighbours they had known for years. Natives who had seemed docile and half-Romanized revealed themselves still barbarians under the skin. There was no chance now to send away the women and children. The whole countryside was in revolt.

Boudicca swept into the town with her frenzied horde of warriors. The Romans barricaded themselves inside the massive new temple of Claudius, the one building that gave them any hope of protection until the relief force from Lincoln could arrive. Boudicca's men proceeded to burn and loot the town. Many peaceful Britons were massacred as their homes went up in flames. They had collaborated with the detested conquerors. They paid the price.

The Roman settlers themselves, though, were the main target for vengeance. For two days the besiegers yelled and battered vainly against the temple walls. They had neither the rams and giant catapults nor the skill as sappers that would have enabled a Roman force to demolish such solid masonry. The temple had no windows and its stout metal-

36

bound doors were backed by heaped-up barricades within.

There was only one way to overwhelm the defenders. Some of Boudicca's men clambered on to the roof, tore off the tiles, and set the beams ablaze. Burning timbers crashed down upon the defenders and the exultant Britons hurled javelins and other missiles. Trapped in that fiery hell, the Romans tried to fight their way out. It was hopeless. Men, women and children were butchered in the colonnade, on the steps, or in the forecourt. Others were dragged to the sacred groves outside the town and sacrificed to the Celtic gods, their heads hacked off and their bodies horribly mutilated.

Boudicca stood triumphant amid the smoking ruins. But Petilius Cerealis was approaching with several thousand men, heavy-armed legionaries with the usual supporting units of horsemen and light infantry. Boudicca and her chieftains had provided for this obvious move. They knew which way the Romans would come. A separate British force laid an ambush. In his anxiety to reach Colchester before it was too late, the Roman commander blundered into the trap. On all sides the myriad Britons rose to view, in such overwhelming numbers that even the trained legionaries could not beat them off. The Roman infantry were wiped out. Only the horsemen, Petilius Cerealis among them, managed to hack their way through the melée and gallop back along the road to Lincoln.

Another notable Roman was also making for safety. Catus Decianus, the tax official who had been so harsh to the Iceni, was in London when the news arrived of what the Queen had done in Colchester. He hurried aboard a ship with his staff and sailed promptly to the Continent.

Meanwhile Suetonius Paulinus had triumphantly completed his mission in North Wales.

He had quelled resistance in the mountainous region of Snowdon. Then, collecting a fleet of shallow-draught landing craft, he had forced the crossing of the Menai Straits and leapt ashore on the Druids' island-refuge of Anglesey. The Druids had been there to meet him, stirring their followers to a frenzy with their weird incantations, while black-robed women wailed and brandished torches. But the Romans cared nothing for their magic. Man or woman, priest or warrior, all were barbarians, defying the imperial majesty of Rome. If they stood in the way, they could expect the same treatment—the murderous jab of the short Roman sword, the crash of the heavy shield-boss. So Anglesey had been taken, and the sacred groves had been cut down like the men who had worshipped there, and the altars of the old Celtic gods had been overthrown.

Then came the shattering news of Colchester, two hundred and fifty miles away. The Governor's first thought was to save London. He set out with his cavalry, leaving his legionaries to march after him as fast as they could. He sent a dispatch-rider to Poenius Postumus who commanded the Second Legion at Gloucester. This force was to cut across the Midlands and meet him on his road to London, thus making up for his own infantry who by then would be plodding several days' journey in his rear.

He reached the appointed meeting-place. But there was no sign of the Second Legion. Poenius Postumus had ignored the order, perhaps because he dared not turn his back on the fierce tribesmen of South Wales. Later realizing that he had made the wrong decision and would be disgraced, this officer committed suicide.

Suetonius Paulinus was of tougher fibre. He shrugged his shoulders and rode forward without the infantry he had relied upon. Soon London lay before him, not safe but as yet untouched by the rebels. The new bridge stretched across the Thames, the trading ships lined the wharfs, the smoke curling above the rooftops was only innocent smoke from kitchen fires and bath-houses.

But Boudicca was coming. Her host was on the march again. It had taken her some time to rally her men after the wild orgies of looting and murder at Colchester, for the Britons did not take kindly to discipline, and she could not rap out her orders like a Roman. What got them moving now was the knowledge that there was nothing more to be done amid the blood-spattered ruins. In London, on the other hand, were the warehouses of the Italian and Gallic merchants, stocked with fine goods imported from the Continent.

London, in fact, was purely a trading city. It had no walls, no garrison of any size. Small wonder that Catus Decianus had fled in panic. Against a host like Boudicca's, and without a legion or two, London was indefensible.

Even the Governor saw that with cavalry alone he could do nothing. Grimly he announced that he was going to withdraw again. Those civilians who could keep up with his column should do so. The rest must save themselves as best they could.

Once Boudicca had got her army moving, she had little more than fifty miles to cover. But, though the chief warriors used fast, lightly-built chariots like her own to carry them to battle, she had no organized cavalry squadrons to make quick advances and her rank-and-file were not trained, like the legions, to keep up a steady pace. Her host did not march, they walked. Indeed, they sauntered if the mood took them, and straggled. Most of them wanted easy plunder. They would turn aside to sack a farm, whereas a Roman stronghold they would have left untouched in their rear for someone else to cope with. Still, London beckoned them, with the promise of more loot than any other town in the island. So they kept together, more or less, and poured through the Essex forests behind the Queen's chariot.

They missed Suetonius Paulinus. He was riding off to the northwest as they swept into London from the northeast. Again there was an appalling massacre. Probably the London Britons, like those at Colchester, imagined that only foreigners would be harmed. Thinking themselves safe, they hesitated to abandon their homes. Only when the warriors ran in with dripping swords and spears did they realize that anyone who had collaborated with the Romans was doomed.

London burned. The human sacrifices were hideously repeated in the sacred groves. Boudicca had to keep her men at a high pitch of excitement or the host would have begun to melt away. Somehow she must hold it together until the main Roman forces had been destroyed. Men's thoughts must not stray to their homes. Luckily, many had their families with them, trailing behind the army in ox-wagons like a migration of nomads. All this multitude had to be fed. That was another problem for the Queen. The Britons were best as guerrilla fighters in small bands living off the country. They were not used to organizing an elaborate supply system like the Romans. Even when granaries and store-houses were captured, and not wastefully looted or burnt, it was an almost impossible task to arrange orderly transport and distribution, to keep this wandering horde regularly fed and contented.

Boubicca knew she must find Suetonius Paulinus and wipe out his army before hunger dispersed her own warriors. She went after him, up the road that later the Saxons named Watling Street. She burst into another Roman town, Verulamium, now St Albans, and the third chapter of horrors was written in flame and blood. In the three

*Plate Ia:* This relief is thought to be Cleopatra dressed as the goddess Isis. In her right hand she holds the ankh, symbol of life; in her left the sceptre. She is wearing the vulture hood, and a crown formed of a disc (the sun) between horns. This is a conventional Egyptian view of Cleopatra and not an actual portrait.

*Plate Ib:* Coins with heads of Cleopatra and Antony, 32/1 B.C. The smaller coin is a denarius of Roman type, the larger a tetradrachm.

*Plate Ic:* A Roman necklace such as Cleopatra might have worn. Gold set with precious stones.

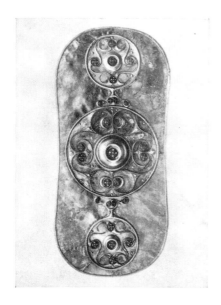

*Plate IIa:* Bronze shield from the Thames at Battersea, probably used during Boudicca's reign.

*Plate IIb:* This carving of a Roman galley is from a temple built by Augustus to celebrate the sea battle of Actium. The crocodile which appears over the ram is a symbol of his victory over Cleopatra the Queen of Egypt. The tower is a miniature fortress erected on the galley from which the soldiers could hurl their darts (hence the word 'forecastle').

massacres about seventy thousand people died, nearly all harmless townsfolk. The population of Roman Britain was only a million.

Nobody knows for certain where Boudicca at last brought the Governor to battle. It was somewhere in the Midlands, where Watling Street slants across the heart of England. The summer was then well advanced. Boudicca's time was running out.

Suetonius Paulinus had mustered a sizeable army. He had the infantry that had followed him from Wales and he had drawn in such other garrisons as he dared to move. Boudicca faced an army of ten thousand Romans, coldly eager to avenge the atrocities of her warriors. Commanding them, she knew, was a veteran general who had proved his skill in Africa as well as in Anglesey.

No hope of surprising this man with an ambush . . . *He* was waiting for *her*. It was she who must advance, she who could not delay. For these Romans would stand or march, patiently obeying orders, as long as they were required to. Her own medley of different tribesmen might break up and drift away as soon as anything went wrong. So, whether she fancied the place or not, she must fight as soon as the Governor offered her the chance.

It is recorded that Suetonius Paulinus chose his ground (wherever precisely it was) on a stretch of heath beside Watling Street. Behind him was a rocky ridge, densely clothed with woodland and cleft by a narrow defile which gave him an ideal centre for his line. Here he massed his heavy infantry, nearly two legions, rank upon rank, with light infantry and cavalry as usual on the wings. Even if these were overwhelmed by the tide of Britons, his flanks would still be protected by the wooded slopes.

Boudicca's host faced them, a turbulent and multi-coloured array in their tartan cloaks and barbaric ornaments, each tribal detachment clustered behind its chiefs, who towered conspicuously in their fantastic helmets. Some, like the Queen herself, stood up in their chariots, clutching their javelins. In the rear stretched the long column of loot-stuffed wagons, from which the women and children hoped to watch the final obliteration of the Romans.

Stridently she harangued her followers. 'Let us show these Romans,' she is said to have urged them, 'that they are hares and foxes trying to rule over hounds and wolves!' Meanwhile, Suetonius Paulinus gave his legionaries terse, practical instructions. 'Throw your javelins. Then stab with your swords and hit them with the shield-boss. Mow them down. Forget about plunder. Win the fight—then it's all yours.'

The battle began. The light chariots raced across the heath towards the wall of shields. They wheeled skilfully, the chieftains threw their spears, the horses sped away again. The Roman mass did not budge. This was mere skirmishing, a way for the chieftains to show off their prowess and insult their enemies.

Now came the serious business. The long trumpets brayed. With blood-curdling howls the main body of Britons started forward. The chiefs leaped down from their chariots, brandishing their long swords, and led the charge on foot.

Still the Romans did not move. Their narrowed eyes peered over their shield-rims, under their peaked helmets. Boudicca had never seen a big Roman force in action. She had heard often enough of their victories in the early years of the invasion, but this incredible quiet restraint, so different from the hysterical fury of her own men, was something that had to be seen for oneself.

The Britons surged on like a spring tide. Then at last came the Roman signal. There was a swish, and over the heads of their front rank came a blizzard of seven-foot javelins. A few moments later came another.

The Roman javelin was cunningly designed. If it struck flesh—the ordinary British warrior had little armour—the hard steel point penetrated deeply. But if it missed completely, or buried its point in a harder surface like the reinforced leather shields of Boudicca's men, there was a joint deliberately made of weaker iron. The spear-point bent but did not snap. The javelin that hit the ground could not be thrown back, while if it stuck in a shield it was like a sting that could not be got rid of, a heavy seven-foot sting that made the shield unusable.

Two such volleys had a devastating effect upon the first wave of Britons. Then, at a fresh order, the Romans began to move forward, shoulder to shoulder, leaving just elbow-room enough to jab with their short swords. They were deceptive, those swords. They looked less dangerous than the longer weapons with which the Britons slashed and hacked. But the Roman, with his peaked and crested helmet, his flexible cuirass of overlapping metal scales, and even his leg-guards, was difficult to wound with an edged blade. He, for his part, could kill with no more than a two-inch poke, delivered in the right spot. He was trained to know the vulnerable places.

So, to her dismay, Boudicca saw the legionaries driving like a wedge into the wavering crowd before them. That her men outnumbered the Romans meant nothing: it merely gave the Romans more to kill. Soon the ground was littered with corpses. The hobnailed legionaries trampled over them. As the Britons died, others in the rear crowded forward. They did not lack courage, only the right training and equipment.

The work of blood went on a long time. Suetonius Paulinus, choosing his moment, unleashed his light infantry and his cavalry to charge in from the flanks. Some slipped round to the rear of the British wagons, slaughtering the oxen or cutting the harness so that the vehicles could not be driven away. What had been grandstands for the Britons' supporters became an immovable barrier, blocking their escape. Hemmed in by the ring of swords, the Britons were pushed back yard by yard against that barrier. They died in their thousands, with many of their women and children. The Romans took no prisoners. They remembered the three cities and what had happened in the sacred groves.

Boudicca drove from the field. She passed, that day, out of history and into legend. Did she commit suicide soon afterwards? It is likely enough. She had nothing to hope for. And she, no more than Cleopatra, was the type of woman to give in meekly and allow herself to be paraded in a Roman triumph. Certainly she did not live long after the battle.

Her gamble had utterly failed. It had cost countless lives and the most ghastly destruction. The Romans were more completely masters of Britain than before. Yet perhaps her rebellion had some good results. The Emperor demanded to know why it had happened. Suetonius Paulinus was censured for allowing the conditions that had caused it and for punishing the population too severely after it was put down. He was recalled, and thenceforward Britain received a succession of humane governors who did much to make the island prosperous. One was that very Petilius Cerealis of the Ninth Legion, who had escaped from the ambush on the Lincoln road.

## THE YEARS BETWEEN 61–390

Between Boudicca's death and the birth of Galla Placidia lie more than three centuries—almost as wide a gap as separates us today from the Pilgrim Fathers—so it is not surprising that the Roman Empire changed greatly in that period. The power was no longer handed down to the descendants of the early Caesars. Often the new emperor was a general who seized that power for himself, or was offered it by the soldiers. He might not be even a true Italian. He might come from Spain, Illyria or North Africa. Rome herself, though still a splendid city and the wonder of the world, ceased to be the capital. With vast dominions now stretching from Scotland to the Sahara and from Portugal to the fringe of Persia, it was easier to govern from Milan, or Trier (now in Germany), or Byzantium (now Istanbul) which Constantine the Great called 'New Rome'. Some emperors felt it was no task for one man: they chose trusted generals as co-emperors, one ruling the western provinces while the other took care of the eastern. Placidia's father, Theodosius the Great, was the last emperor to rule single-handed. It was he, too, who just before her birth made Christianity the official religion.

Many dangers and problems afflicted the emperors. There were the barbarians, forever pounding against the frontiers like a flood-tide, Goths, Vandals, Franks, Lombards, and many others, pressing forward from the plains and forests of northeastern Europe. Many had picked up a degree of civilization and were glad enough to serve the Empire as soldiers. They claimed to be Christians, though they followed the teachings of a heretic, Arius, and were disapproved of by ordinary churchmen. Some of these warriors were promoted to high posts in the Roman Army, but others led the attacks upon it. Behind these semi-civilized tribes loomed a darker peril from the steppes of Central Asia—the ruthless Huns, a horde of heathen nomads.

This then was the position of the ancient Roman Empire, stretched to the limit, overgrown and unwieldy, harassed by enemies, like some prehistoric monster that had outlived its epoch, when Galla Placidia was born.

# 3. Galla Placidia, the Empress in the West

Her father was without question the mightiest man in all the world.

She sensed it, young though she was, as she moved wide-eyed through those palaces of incomparable splendour. His bodyguard were like living statues, armoured and glittering from head to foot, their faces invisible within their helmet-masks. His standards were like purple dragons, rippling and hissing as they strained in the breeze.

She was called Galla Placidia. Galla was the name of her mother, whose beauty also she inherited. Her mother's mother too, the Empress Justina, had been reputed one of the loveliest women of her generation. The second name, Placidia, was an ironical choice, for her life was to be anything but placid. Danger and adventure, conspiracy and conflict, would be its main ingredients.

She was born about A.D. 390 (the exact year is uncertain) and as it chanced she was born in Rome, though it was seldom now that the emperors visited the former capital. Only civil war and disorder in Italy had brought Theodosius into the peninsula at all. Born in Spain, he had served as a soldier in Britain, and since becoming emperor had spent most of his time in the eastern provinces, defending the Danube frontier against the barbarians. But being in Italy he had seized the opportunity to celebrate his victories with an old-style triumph in Rome. Most likely Placidia's birth fell in the following year.

Theodosius had been married before. Placidia had two half-brothers, Arcadius and Honorius. For those first years the whole family remained in Italy, though to so small a child one palace must have looked much like any other, with the same crowds of servants and soldiers, even the same hangings and furniture transported from place to place. She saw little of her father, for he was busy reorganizing the government of Italy and fighting battles in the north.

That early family life ended all too soon. In 394 Placidia's mother died. In September of that year her father came back to Rome after yet another victory. There were great rejoicings and she saw her second half-brother, Honorius, proclaimed 'Augustus'. Arcadius already had the title: it meant that their father intended them to be co-emperors, perhaps helping him when they were old enough, certainly following him when he died. Arcadius was already eighteen, Honorius only eleven.

Placidia was no more than a very little girl. She did not count. It did not seem likely that she ever would.

Early the next year Theodosius died in Milan. By his will he appointed Arcadius Emperor in the East, ruling from Byzantium, and Honorius Emperor in the West, with his capital in Milan. Arcadius was to be guided by his tutor, Rufinus, and Honorius was made the ward of his father's trusted general, Stilicho. This Stilicho was actually a barbarian, a Vandal, but long and faithful service in the imperial armies had civilized him. He was a fine general, and Theodosius knew he was the best man to defend the Empire against invaders. Also, just because he was a barbarian, he could never become emperor himself, so he would not be tempted to betray the boy put into his charge.

Placidia's future was no problem. She would go with Arcadius and be brought up in his court at Byzantium.

47

For the next few years she spent her days in the palace that was almost a city in itself, rising from the blue waters of the Bosphorus.

It was a place of fantastic splendour. Her brother gave audience in a hall with a golden ceiling, supported by columns of silver and gold. There was more gold on the cedarwood furniture. What was not precious metal was shimmering marble of various tints, green from Carystus, white from the nearby Sea of Marmora, deep red and silver and rose from Phrygia, together with porphyry and other coloured stone from Greece, Asia Minor and even distant Africa.

Arcadius sat on a jewelled and gilded throne, with a canopy supported by the spread wings of four eagles, each perched on a pillar. No youth could sit there without feeling something like a god. On all sides there was flattery. The Emperor was referred to as 'Lord of the Universe' or 'Our Master, the Eternal and Ever August Arcadius'. He spoke grandly of himself as 'Our Clemency' or 'My Eternity'. His house was 'the Sacred Palace'. 'Royal' or 'Imperial' was not enough, everything about him was 'Sacred'. His courtiers and officials were graded in ranks, each with its privileges and titles, and woe betide any careless underling who said 'Most Honourable' to some minister who rated as 'Illustrious'.

It was now, rather than in her father's time, that Placidia learned what it meant to be an emperor. Yet Theodosius had been truly 'Great', a brilliant man who had reached the throne on merit, invited into partnership by the Emperor Gratian. Arcadius was merely his father's son, and beneath the gorgeous Byzantine robes breathed an insignificant young man, easily managed by his ministers or by the girl he married, Eudoxia, daughter of another of his father's barbarian commanders, Bauto the Frank.

That was another lesson Placidia learned at Byzantium. The imperial power could be manipulated by a woman. If there was no emperor of her father's calibre available, an able woman was better than an ineffective man.

It was fortunate for her own character that she did not remain too long in the stifling air of that semi-Oriental court, with its rigid rules and ceremonial, its abject worship of authority.

When she was about seven she was taken back to Italy, not to her other brother's court at Milan but to Rome, to live with the dowager Empress Laeta, widow of Gratian. Laeta was a kindly, elderly lady, deeply religious, lavishing much of her wealth on the city poor. In her villa on the Aventine Hill, the fashionable quarter for Rome's thousand leading families, Placidia found a happy home for the remainder of her girlhood.

This Rome in which she grew up was even more majestic than the city Cleopatra had seen four centuries earlier.

In actual power, true, it was a mere shadow of the place that Julius Caesar had dominated. There was still a Senate, there were officials with old traditional names, but they counted for little. The Emperor ruled from other capitals. And the power of the Pope lay still in the future— the Bishop of Rome enjoyed special prestige as the successor of St Peter, but he was not yet the political figure that he later became.

To the eye, however, Rome was undiminished in glory. For four hundred years successive emperors had improved and beautified the city. Palaces and villas, theatres and triumphal arches, public gardens and fountains, baths and lecture-halls and libraries, great island blocks of dwellings, and temples (now being converted to Christian churches) were all enclosed within the thirteen-mile circuit of the

Aurelian Walls, forming a city of perhaps a million and a quarter inhabitants.

Strangely enough, those walls, begun by the Emperor Aurelian in A.D. 271, and so outwardly impressive with their sixty-foot ramparts, their fourteen fortified gates, their massive square towers at frequent intervals, were a sign not of Rome's strength but of her weakness. In the old days she had needed no walls like these. No foreign army had come within hundreds of miles of the city. Now, no one could be sure. One day, those walls might be badly needed.

In early times Roman power had been built up by true Romans, like Caesar. Now that stock had degenerated. The born Romans, the native Italians even, indeed their long-civilized and 'Romanized' neighbours in countries like Gaul—these counted for little by A.D. 400. Had they but known it, the Empire had already yielded to the barbarians. It was the armies enlisted from the more Romanized barbarians that now held the frontiers against the wilder ones outside. The generals were barbarian chiefs. Theodosius himself had been unable to do without them. There had been Bauto the Frank, whose daughter married Arcadius. There was Stilicho the Vandal, appointed Honorius's guardian: *his* daughter Maria was soon married to Honorius, and, when she died, the weak young Emperor was induced to marry her younger sister, Thermantia. Placidia, perhaps unfairly, hated Stilicho and all his brood. She saw them dominating her brother and using her father's will to inherit the Empire. East or West, it was a similar story.

Theodosius had had a third barbarian general, however, Alaric the Goth—and Alaric was far from pleased to be the one left out of this division.

The Goths were originally Scandinavians who had wandered south through Germany—a warrior people, riding ahead of the wagon-trains that carried their families and possessions. Alaric had mixed with Romans, seen Athens and Byzantium, been at court, served under imperial command, been baptized a Christian of the Arian kind, holding that God the Son was somehow separate from, and subordinate to, God the Father. But at heart Alaric remained a nomadic barbarian, believing himself descended from the pagan gods of Valhalla.

Disappointed by the turn affairs had taken, Alaric told his men: 'The Goths have fought Rome's battles long enough. It is time to fight their own.' His warriors lifted him on their shields in the traditional manner and acclaimed him King of the Goths. He led them across the Alps into Italy.

Stilicho was a match for his fellow-barbarian. He surprised and routed the Gothic army on Easter Sunday, in the year A.D. 400. Alaric retired from Italy, but not forever. He was still a young man, ambitious and determined on revenge. Wisely, Stilicho moved the young Emperor and his court from the exposed city of Milan to Ravenna, amid the marshes on the Adriatic coast. It seemed to many a cowardly move. Probably Placidia thought so. But Stilicho knew what he was doing. No Gothic army could penetrate the maze of canals and morasses round Ravenna, but his own troops could always come out and fight. Ravenna barred the road to Rome and had unbroken sea-communications with Byzantium. It was no skulking-place but a springboard for action.

Stilicho was the one man who might have saved Rome. But his son-in-law had come to hate him, as young rulers often hate the strong men who have been their guardians. Honorius was a flabby, effeminate coward, showing determination only in the persecution of those who did not share his strict religious beliefs. He would not give State employment to heretics or to pagans, although many of the ablest men in the Empire had not yet accepted Christianity, and in this way he lost the services of officers he could ill spare. Apart from his devotions, he was chiefly interested in raising chickens, a harmless but rather odd occupation for the ruler of an imperiled empire. Though twice married, he had no children.

Not man enough to assert himself against Stilicho, Honorius schemed to remove him. Stilicho sought sanctuary in a church at Ravenna, was lured outside, and put to death. There was no one then capable of stopping Alaric.

The Goths descended upon Italy again. They ravaged the North, marched southwards and blockaded Rome. Honorius stayed safe amid the marshes of Ravenna. He would not—perhaps could not—lift a finger to defend the ancient capital. Alaric, without the complicated siege-engines of the Roman Army, could never break down the fortifications. He could starve the citizens, though. For centuries Rome's vast population had depended on corn shipped from North Africa. It was easy to stop that food entering the city.

Placidia saw the corpses lying in the streets, where people had died of hunger. Laeta used her money generously to buy what food she could (there were as always unscrupulous hoarders and speculators, making profit out of death) and Placidia helped her to distribute it among the poor.

In the end a bargain was struck with Alaric. He was paid a large sum of ransom money to go away. But soon, having failed to secure a permanent arrangement with Honorius (he was asking for land where his tribe could settle in what is now Yugoslavia), he came back and blockaded Rome again. The second ransom was larger. The Senate had to pay him five thousand pounds of gold and thirty thousand of silver, and they promised to persuade the Emperor, if they could, to make a reasonable agreement.

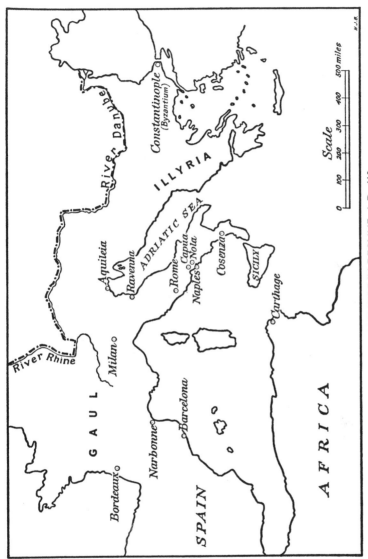

THE ROMAN EMPIRE IN DECLINE, A.D. 410
The frontier no longer held back the Barbarians.

Honorius remained stubborn. From his own safe refuge he sent an insulting refusal. Alaric marched south again to besiege Rome. One August night in 410 (the year from which we commonly date the fall of the Roman Empire) Placidia heard distant shouting and saw the glow of fire in the sky near the Salarian Gate.

The Goths were inside the city. For the first time since Rome's sack by the Gauls in 390 B.C., exactly eight centuries earlier, the greatest city in the world had fallen to a foreign assailant.

Resistance was brief and feeble. Rome had no troops fit to stand against these stalwart northerners. It was a night of terror. Some houses were set on fire to light up the scene for the invaders as they began their looting. Servants turned against unpopular masters and joined in the pillage. The city criminals, as always on such occasions, emerged from their haunts and made good use of their chances.

Placidia found herself a prisoner, which, in that turmoil, was the best fate that could have befallen her. She was safe from harm and she was honourably treated. Alaric knew her value. She was the Emperor's half-sister, a hostage to bargain with.

Day dawned on a spectacle of confusion. Smoke drifted across the city, acrid with the tang of smouldering timber. Here and there lay bodies, some dead, some merely dead drunk. Wagons came creaking in through the gates, crammed with wide-eyed barbarian families. They pitched camp in the spacious squares and settled down as though in some clearing in their native pine-forests. The warriors were still breaking down the doors of the wealthier houses and emerging with plunder. Magnificent bronze statues were carried off to the melting-pot. Exquisite glass and pottery were wantonly smashed on the pavement.

54

Alaric and his chieftains did what they could to control their followers, but for the moment it was not much. The Goths were a wild, free people. They chose their own leaders and they would take no orders that seemed to them unreasonable. Gold, bronze, silk, wine: such things they could understand. But art, books, architecture, all this elaborate meaningless culture—what use was it? One thing, though, they did understand: they too were Christians, and those who looted churches of sacred vessels and relics were robbing God. So, when the order ran round to respect Christian buildings and take Church property into safe-keeping, the Goths obeyed. The Bishop of Rome was absent from the city: Innocent I, as he was later reckoned in the roll of popes, was away at the Emperor's court in Ravenna.

Placidia found Alaric's headquarters an oasis of comparative sanity amid all this turmoil. There was order and decency, not the uncouthness of a savage encampment as she might have feared. Alaric knew Roman ways and how to behave. So did his close comrades, men like his wife's brother, Ataulf, whose name meant 'Son of a Wolf' but who seemed relatively civilized and agreeable. There was even a bishop, Sigesarius, an Arian heretic admittedly, but at a time like that any kind of bishop provided some reassurance.

After the first panic, Placidia recovered her nerve. She was safe with Alaric, she reckoned. If anything happened to her, he would lose a useful bargaining counter. But she would be unwise to trade on that too far. There was no point in offending the Goths. She might as well make herself pleasant to them. She could keep her dignity without being haughty. It was not difficult, with her youth and good looks, to charm her captors.

The Goths stayed only three days in the city. It was food they needed and Rome had never enough to feed the population, let alone a horde of invaders with wives and children. So Alaric called a halt to the looting. He would lead them south. If necessary, they would seize ships and sail across to Africa where the corn came from.

The destruction had been nothing compared with what Rome was to suffer later. But A.D. 410 is the date that blazes through history. This was the first time, the year when the world learned with stunned horror that Rome *could* be taken by barbarians. It was the year from which we commonly date the beginning of the misnamed 'Dark Ages' and the end of Roman Britain, though the legions had in fact been withdrawn from the island a year or two earlier.

At the end of August the Goths rode out through the gates, their faces to the south, their endless columns of waggons trundling after them along the straight paved road.

With them went their imperial prisoner, Placidia.


Slowly, that autumn, the host made its way down the Italian peninsula. The Goths captured Nola and Capua, but were repulsed from Naples. They were not all-conquering. When resistance was strong enough, they sheered away. There was plenty of easy plunder in what had been Rome's most luxurious resorts. Placidia lodged in splendid villas, enjoying as much comfort as ever she had done. Her captors lounged in the shade of plane-tree and cypress, amid fountains and rose-gardens, while their nervous hosts plied them with the best Falernian wine in gem-crusted goblets. If the girl ever considered escape, she dismissed the idea. Where could she escape to? She would find a cool welcome from Honorius in Ravenna: he would be glad to have her out of barbarian hands but only for

*Plate IIIa:* The Mausoleum of Galla Placidia in Ravenna. The building is in the shape of a cross, the four arms meeting in a central dome.

*Plate IIIb:* The Good Shepherd mosaic inside Galla Placidia's mausoleum.

*Plate IV:* Isabella the Catholic: statue in the Sacristy of the
Royal Chapel.

state reasons, not for her own sake. And Byzantium? Her brother Arcadius was dead, his small son sat on the throne beneath the eagle canopy, and what place was there for a young fugitive aunt? Neither the imperial ladies of Byzantium nor their scheming ministers wanted an intruder in their narrow world.

Placidia adapted herself to the roving life of the Goths. She made friends especially with Ataulf. He was a fine-looking man, though not as tall as his brother-in-law. He was intelligent and popular. He was Alaric's right-hand man, entrusted with great responsibilities.

He had entered Italy only the previous year, she learned. He had brought reinforcements to Alaric from the outer lands along the Danube. At first, he frankly confessed, he had thought only of overthrowing Rome and setting up a Gothic empire in its place. But the more he saw of Italy and the complicated wonders of Roman civilization—the roads, aqueducts, bridges, harbours, post-houses, and all the smooth-running administration that kept life going, even in those disturbed days, for millions of people—the more he realized that it was something to be preserved and something the Goths themselves could not preserve. They did not understand how it worked. So Rome must carry on, run by the people who *did* understand, but with the warrior Goths to rule and protect and inject new vitality.

That was Ataulf's vision. Alaric's ideas, unfortunately, were rooted in the past. He was the mighty chief of a nomad horde, seeking land for his tribe. He saw no further. And Alaric, not Ataulf, was king.

They reached the toe of Italy. A fleet of galleys was assembled. They would cross to North Africa, then the fertile granary of the western empire. If they liked it there they would settle, carving out a new Gothland on the edge of the Sahara. And if not. . . .

Alaric never had to answer that question. A storm wrecked his fleet before he could embark. He marched north again to make another attempt on Naples: he could muster a second fleet there. But at Cosenza, a little town in Calabria, he was stricken with fever and died.

Then Placidia witnessed the strange burial of a barbarian king. At moments like this the Christianity of the Goths wore very thin. Hundreds of slaves toiled to dig a channel and build a dam, diverting the course of the River Busento. In the manner of his heathen ancestors, Alaric was laid splendidly to rest, surrounded by treasures he would need in the next world, his grave dug in the former river-bed. Then the dam was demolished, and the muddy waters frothed back into their old course, hiding the spot forever.

Now the Goths had to choose a new leader and with one voice they shouted for Ataulf, the Son of the Wolf. Ataulf was raised shoulder high upon their shields and acclaimed 'King of the Goths'.

It was an event in which Placidia had a special interest. From what happened in the next year or two it is clear that she and Ataulf were by this time falling genuinely in love.

What was to be the next move?

To Ataulf and Placidia there seemed an obvious answer. The Goths had the fighting men, the Empire had everything else—land, wealth, organization. As allies, they could face all comers. A marriage between the Gothic king and the Emperor's sister would seal that alliance. Emperors had taken barbarian wives, why should not their sisters take barbarian husbands?

That was the proposition submitted to Honorius. Alone, he might have agreed to it, but he was now much under the influence of his new commander-in-chief, Constantius, an

Illyrian who had served in many campaigns under Theodosius. Constantius was middle-aged but had ambitions still to satisfy. The suggested marriage would ruin his own schemes. He persuaded Honorius to refuse. Placidia was left at the mercy of the Goths. Honorius and Constantius could not rescue her, but they would not agree to her marrying Ataulf.

Ataulf and Placidia went their way just the same. Since the Goths could not stay in Italy, because of the food problem, Ataulf led them over the Alps into Gaul, where a usurper named Jovinus had set up in opposition to Honorius. Ataulf defeated Jovinus and sent his head to Ravenna, hoping that this helpful action would make the Emperor more friendly. It had no particular effect. Honorius went on feeding his hens at Ravenna and avoiding his larger responsibilities.

In January, 414, Ataulf and Placidia decided to wait no longer for her brother's consent. They were married at Narbonne, then a Mediterranean port, on the coast that sweeps round to Spain and the Pyrenees.

It was a splendid wedding in the old Roman style, not in a church but in the mansion of a leading Narbonne citizen. Bishop Sigesarius performed the service. The bride, robed in all the magnificence of her imperial rank, sat on a throne of state. Ataulf, his Gothic furs exchanged for a fine Roman tunic, was content with an ordinary seat beside her. A choir chanted a bridal song and fifty handsome youths in silken robes filed up to Placidia and offered her wedding gifts. In each hand they carried bowls, one filled with gold pieces, the other with jewels. The offering was a Gothic custom, but the gold and jewels had been plundered from the Empire.

This was the happiest period in Placidia's life, but it was all too short.

The marriage did not produce the desired alliance. Instead, Honorius sent an army against them, under Constantius. He had troops now—the position was always changing, almost from day to day, as armies mutinied or returned to their allegiance, or fresh barbarians were hired. Europe was sliding into chaos. With only scanty records, the modern historian cannot build up a detailed picture at every stage. But clearly Constantius was now strong enough to be a menace even to the Goths. He advanced on Bordeaux, where Ataulf and Placidia were holding court. The Goths retreated into Spain.

Now Placidia bore a son, baptized Theodosius after his famous grandfather. Surely Honorius would see reason now? He had no son himself, no likelihood of any. What better heir to the Empire than his sister's boy?

But the infant Theodosius died soon after the Goths had found themselves a new resting-place at Barcelona. He was buried in a silver coffin amid general lamentation. Death was familiar, however, and babies perished as numerously as soldiers in battle. Placidia was young and strong. She looked forward to giving Ataulf other sons.

There was no time for that. Ataulf, like any Gothic leader, had made enemies. One such enemy, Sarus, he had killed, so starting a blood-feud. On an autumn day in 415, as he walked through his stables at Barcelona, he was stabbed in the back by a groom who had been a follower of Sarus. Ataulf's dying thought was of Placidia. 'Strive to live in peace with Rome,' he whispered to his followers, 'and hand back Placidia to the Emperor.'

Ataulf's successor cared nothing for his dying wishes. Power was seized by his bitterest enemy, Singeric, brother of Sarus. Singeric dared not put Placidia to death, but he humiliated her brutally. He made her march twelve miles, bound like a slave, beside one of his troopers.

The usurper lasted only seven days. Then Ataulf's old comrades rallied and killed him. Walia was proclaimed King of the Goths. Almost his first act was to fulfil Ataulf's instructions. A treaty was this time agreed with the Emperor. Placidia was escorted to the foothills of the Pyrenees, where Constantius received her with impressive ceremonial. The Goths were given 600,000 measures of corn. Placidia set off for her brother's court at Ravenna. That chapter in her life was closed.

The long-term scheme of Constantius began to unfold.

It was to become co-emperor. Marriage to Honorius's sister—possible now that she was a widow and no longer with the Gothic army—was an essential step in the scheme.

Honorius had privately promised him that, if by any means he could get Placidia out of barbarian hands, such a marriage would be given every encouragement. Placidia herself, though, felt no enthusiasm.

Constantius was hardly a young woman's romantic ideal, but throughout history few royal marriages have been arranged on a romantic basis. He was a good deal older than Placidia. His massive head was set on a thick neck, his eyes bulged, and though he could be charming at times, he often wore a sulky expression. Certainly he was a strong character and an effective general and cut an impressive figure at court, though he could lay aside his dignity and even play the fool at parties.

Gradually Placidia's opposition was worn down. She was not, after all, a modern girl with freedom to choose. She knew that if ever she was to enjoy married life again, she must take the husband her brother offered. So in 417, on the day when by ancient but now empty tradition two 'consuls' took office—in this case Honorius himself for the eleventh time and Constantius for the second—the betrothal was publicly signified by the Emperor's taking his sister's hand and placing it in his colleague's.

The wedding was celebrated with immense pomp. Constantius wanted to blot out the memory of that earlier wedding in Narbonne. After a visit to Rome with Honorius, they returned to Ravenna.

The city, now to be Placidia's home for so many years, lay in a flat landscape with only a ridge of far-off mountains to break the horizon. Sea and land, marsh, lagoon and waterway, formed one dead level, haunted by frogs and mosquitoes. A causeway linked the city with the naval base of Classis, three miles distant, where two or three hundred galleys could anchor. Boatmen, poling flat-bottomed marsh craft, glided hither and thither through the town, like forerunners of the gondoliers in a Venice that did not yet exist. There was water everywhere, but little fit to drink. Though safe as a refuge, Ravenna was inconvenient as a home. The imperial court made the best of it. Palaces and churches were rising. The foundations were laid of the city whose art treasures still, in some degree, survive.

In due time Placidia bore a daughter, Honoria, and in the following year a son, Valentinian. In the fourth year of their marriage Constantius attained his ambition: reluctantly Honorius agreed to make him co-emperor. Placidia assumed the proud title of Augusta.

Wife of one emperor, sister of the other, she was now at the hub of power. She saw how the government worked, came to know the leading ministers—the Imperial Chamberlain, the Chancellor, the Praetorian Prefect, the Supreme Commander and the Master of the Offices, who controlled not only the whole elaborate civil service but also the Secret Police. She was careful to build up a household of people faithful to herself, from her own Grand Chamberlain down to her waiting-women and the children's nurse.

Her bodyguard were Goths, fiercely loyal. The tall northern warriors strode proudly through Ravenna, sometimes coming to blows with the imperial soldiers they despised.

Constantius was not particularly enjoying the throne he had worked so long to win. He had been snubbed by the Emperor in the East, or rather by that youth's elder sister, Pulcheria, who was the true ruler at Byzantium. In theory the Empire was still one, the two courts acting in harmony. Statues of Constantius should have been set up in Byzantium, but when they were shipped there from Ravenna they were not accepted. The twenty-year-old Byzantine Emperor, Theodosius II, ignored his uncle's choice of a colleague.

In Ravenna, on the other hand, Constantius chafed at the stiff etiquette that bound him. He sighed for the free-and-easy life he had lived before he became a 'sacred' and 'eternal' ruler. His nerves suffered. He was troubled by dreams. He had a feeling that he had not long to live. It was a true premonition. Death came, through inflammation of the lungs, only seven months after he had been hailed as Emperor.

So, in her early thirties, Placidia found herself a widow for the second time. Honorius was once more alone. Could she guide her weak brother, as Pulcheria controlled *her* brother at Byzantium? Only, it seemed, at a price she could not pay. For now the degenerate Honorius developed an odd affection for his beautiful half-sister and began to behave as if they were not related at all, embarrassing her in public with his embraces. This might have done at the court of the Ptolemies. It would not do for Placidia.

Taking her two small children, she embarked in a ship and fled to Byzantium.

She was back where she had been a quarter of a century earlier: an unwanted female relative, an embarrassment to her nephew and the jealous women who dominated him.

In the meantime she had known the wide world. As Ataulf's queen she had roved the breadth of Western Europe to the Atlantic coast. After such freedom the narrow life at Ravenna had been bad enough. Byzantium was stifling.

Pulcheria and her sisters, Arcadia and Marina, had turned their brother's palace into something more like a convent, where no men were welcome except their chaplains. Pulcheria's marriage was an empty form. The three young women had publicly dedicated their virginity to God. They lived like nuns. For several hours, each day and night, they chanted psalms and recited prayers. They fasted, despised fine clothes, and gave up their time to Church embroidery.

The Emperor in the East was as devout as his sisters. Apart from hunting, he pursued blameless indoor hobbies such as painting, carving and calligraphy. Being a man, he had been allowed and encouraged to marry. Pulcheria had just chosen a bride for him, a slim, golden-haired, fair-skinned Athenian named Eudocia, as intellectual as she was beautiful: although of pagan origin, she was able to please her sister-in-law by turning the first eight books of the Old Testament into fluent verse. But when it came to managing Theodosius, Pulcheria allowed no competition. She had conditioned her brother to be no more than a dignified figurehead, grave, unsmiling, ever saying the right thing. In the background Pulcheria, brilliant and unscrupulous, pulled the strings but allowed him to enjoy the shows of majesty.

In this cloistered court the fugitive Placidia might easily have ended her days, sunk without trace, but there was a sudden new reversal of her circumstances. Word came from Ravenna in September, 423: Honorius had died of dropsy and his throne had been seized by one of his leading ministers, Joannes.

This was more than the imperial family at Byzantium could stand. Ministers must not be allowed to do these things. It was far worse than the elevation of Constantius, which Byzantium had refused to recognize a year or two before. The upstart Joannes must be overthrown. There was only one thing to do. Placidia must be proclaimed Empress in the West, as regent for her small son, Valentinian, and confirmed in her title of 'Augusta', which previously her nephew and nieces had refused to recognize. She must be given Byzantine forces with which to capture Ravenna. And finally, to tie everything up neatly for the family, as far ahead as anyone could foresee, the four-year-old Valentinian, before leaving, should be formally betrothed to Theodosius's baby daughter, Licinia Eudoxia.

Defeating the usurper proved less easy than expected. Two Byzantine armies were sent out against him, while Placidia herself, with the children, took ship to Aquileia, at the head of the Adriatic whence she could quickly move to Ravenna as soon as the city fell. The ship ran into a violent storm. It looked at one time as though they would be wrecked and either drown or be taken prisoner on a hostile shore. However, their fervent prayers to the Saints appeared to be answered, and they reached Aquileia safely.

Meanwhile came the bad news that one of the Byzantine commanders, Ardaburius, had been taken a prisoner to Ravenna and had changed sides. The first part of the report was true, the second false. Ardaburius was deceiving his captors to gain time. He bribed a man to slip out to his son, who had taken over his command, and guide him through the marshes in a surprise attack upon the city. This succeeded. Joannes was defeated and executed. Placidia entered Ravenna in triumph, saluted on all sides as Augusta, the Empress in the West.

Her wanderings were over, though it would be sadly untrue to say that she lived happily ever after.

For the next fourteen years, while Valentinian grew to manhood, she bore the burden of trying to hold together a handful of provinces that were all the time falling apart. She had to control powerful and ambitious commanders, striving to balance one against another.

At first she had a reliable commander-in-chief named Felix. His rival, Aëtius, had originally backed the usurper, Joannes, then made his peace with Placidia and been rewarded with a post in Gaul. Later, having made himself strong, Aëtius returned, forced Placidia to give him Felix's position, and secured Felix's execution for alleged treason.

A third general, Boniface, was paramount in Africa. He had supported Placidia against Joannes. Now he rebelled and made a deal with the Vandals, sharing his African territory with them. When he fell out with the Vandals, under their astute and treacherous leader, Gaiseric, he fled to Ravenna, leaving them in sole possession, and managed to win Placidia's forgiveness. Doubtless she was eager to use him against Aëtius. She gave him the latter's position and a civil war followed. Boniface won, but shortly afterwards died. Aëtius had taken refuge with Rugila, King of the Huns. Now he came back, and, as Placidia had no one to pit against him, she had no choice but to restore him to his command. Such were the hollow satisfactions of being mistress of the western world. She must have sighed bitterly for the long-dead Ataulf. With a husband like that, how differently she could have coped with her problems!

Her son was little help. Valentinian was weak and spoilt. Horses and archery interested him more than the business of the Empire. He loved pleasure and resented having to cut down his expenditure, but, as Placidia tried to explain to him, with some provinces completely lost, like

Britain, and the revenue much reduced from others, like Gaul and Africa, the Empire was in financial difficulties. Another point at issue between them was Valentinian's fondness for astrologers, whom his devout mother regarded as agents of Satan.

In 437 Valentinian journeyed to Byzantium and married Licinia Eudoxia, now grown into a princess of classic Greek beauty. When he returned, he assumed his full powers as Emperor in the West. Placidia's regency was officially ended. She exerted what influence she could behind the scenes, but Valentinian listened more to her old enemy, Aëtius.

In time Valentinian became the father of two daughters. Both were betrothed while they were almost in the cradle, and for purely political reasons which must have galled their grandmother. One, baptized Placidia after herself, was promised to Olybrius, son of the ambitious Aëtius: years afterwards, the marriage took place and Olybrius became for a few months one of the last inglorious emperors. The other girl, Eudoxia, was assigned to Huneric, son of Gaiseric, King of the Vandals, who had captured Carthage and was building up a navy to threaten Italy by sea.

There was not much Placidia could do now. She was the devout dowager, worshipping in the churches she had built, doing good works as Laeta had taught her to do when a girl in Rome. She helped to make Ravenna the city of Byzantine splendour we can still guess at from the remains. One of the churches she built was to St John the Evangelist, fulfilling a vow she had made when she was so nearly shipwrecked. That alarming adventure was portrayed in brilliant mosaics, the distinctive art form of Byzantium. There are other beautiful mosaics in the so-called 'Mausoleum of Galla Placidia', a cross-shaped building with alabaster windows that is still one of the sights of Ravenna.

She may well have built it, though experts now doubt whether it was her family tomb.

Perhaps her greatest problem in her final years was her daughter, Justa Grata Honoria.

Like herself, Honoria had a strong personality: it seemed that in the imperial family all the vitality went into the women. Throughout her girlhood Honoria enjoyed honour and deference at Court, but once her brother married and had children, her importance began to fade. Having a better brain than Valentinian, she found it irksome to be ignored. It was the same situation that Placidia had had to endure with Honorius. Mother and daughter might naturally have drawn together in sympathy, but something else divided them.

Whom could Honoria marry? She must not take a husband powerful enough to cast eyes on her brother's throne. But she was of imperial blood and could not make an unworthy match.

At thirty-two Honoria was still unmarried, though she had been given her own establishment in the palace. She was not like her pious relatives at Byzantium, happy to dedicate herself to God alone. Forbidden marriage, she developed a love affair with her chamberlain, Eugenius. When the scandal was discovered, the chamberlain was put to death and Honoria was unwillingly betrothed to a rich but dull senator.

Not for nothing was Honoria the daughter of Placidia. She summoned her trusted eunuch, Hyacinthus, handed him a ring, and told him to carry it to Attila, the dreaded King of the Huns, who had ravaged the Empire from Gaul almost to the gates of Byzantium. It was her proposal of marriage.

Attila had no intention of making Honoria his bride, but he was too cunning to refuse outright. Instead, he sent word to Theodosius in Byzantium, as the senior emperor, claiming half Valentinian's western provinces as her dowry. Theodosius actually advised Valentinian to accept and send his sister to the Hunnish leader, but the settlement was never concluded. The hapless Hyacinthus was tortured and beheaded for his part in the business, and it was all Placidia could do to persuade her furious son not to execute his sister as well.

Such were the last sad days of the Empress, with family feuds and scandals matching the greater disorders of the Empire she had tried to save. Had she but known it, the Western Empire had only another twenty-six years to live. Those twenty-six years would see ten more emperors, before the last in the line of nobodies, Romulus Augustulus, was contemptuously pensioned off by the Goths in 476, his regalia conscientiously dispatched to Byzantium as 'no longer required'.

Placidia, who had lived through the decline of the Roman Empire, was spared from seeing its fall. On November 27, 450, she closed her eyes for the last time where she had first opened them, in Rome, which she was even then trying to have restored as the imperial capital it once had been.

## THE YEARS BETWEEN 450–1451

A thousand and one years went by. The Roman Empire in the West collapsed only a generation after Placidia's death. The old clear pattern of imperial provinces was overlaid by a vaguer patchwork of barbarian kingdoms. Gradually some of these took shape as units we recognize today. By the Middle Ages England and France had appeared as distinct nations, but Germany, Italy and Spain remained much longer divided into innumerable smaller states.

In those ten centuries was evolved the feudal system. All rule was on a military basis. The knight in his castle obeyed his lord, and that lord his overlord, and so on up to the king. As women were not expected to ride into battle (Joan of Arc scandalized people by doing so) there was no place in such a system for women to hold political power. They had to exert their influence behind the scenes as best they could, as wives and mothers like Edward III's famous consort, Queen Philippa, or deputize as regents for an absent husband or a youthful son, like the formidable Queen Margaret of Scandinavia. Maud,[1] William the Conqueror's grand-daughter, did claim the full dignity of the English throne for herself, but she found the opposition too strong and in the end had to compromise.

By 1451 Europe was moving out of the Middle Ages into a new era. The battles of Crecy and Agincourt were memories. Cannons were ending the dominance of knight and castle. Trade had grown, merchants and bankers were immensely powerful, notably in Renaissance Italy. Feudalism was on its way out, capitalism on its way in. It was easier to run a strong central government, and there was no logical reason why a woman should not wear the crown if she had loyal councillors and commanders to take her orders. Tradition of course was against her, and prejudice, and in France an actual law, the Salic Law, but sometime, somewhere, it was bound to happen.

It happened in Spain. Isabella of Castile deserves to be remembered for many things, not merely because she gave Columbus his chance, and so was responsible, almost by accident, for the discovery of America. Historically, she is more interesting because of her own dynamic character and career, and because she united Spain.

---

[1] Maud's story is told in *The Seven Queens of England*.

# 4. Isabella of Spain

Isabella was born on April 22, 1451, in a little town with an exquisite name, Madrigal de las Altas Torres—'Madrigal of the High Towers'. It lay northwest of Madrid, which was not yet a city of much importance. Madrigal stood within a ring of brick ramparts built long before by the Moors when they held most of Spain. All around stretched the bleak stony uplands of Avila, the setting of all her childhood.

She was a fair-skinned girl with blue-green eyes and blond hair with coppery lights. Perhaps that was the Plantagenet in her, for on both sides she was descended from John of Gaunt, and so from Edward III and the earlier English kings. In build she was rather stocky.

Her father, Juan II, had been King of Castile for almost half a century. He loved art and music but lacked the toughness a ruler needed in those days. Castile was only one part of Spain but by far the biggest. There was the Kingdom of Navarre at the Atlantic end of the Pyrenees; thence, the much larger Kingdom of Aragon ran along the mountain range to the Mediterranean and halfway down the coast, to include Barcelona and Valencia; in the far south, from Gibraltar to Malaga, Almeria and beyond, the fertile Kingdom of Granada was the last stronghold of the Moors; and on the west lay Portugal. Even alone, Castile was a considerable realm, but it needed a stronger ruler than Juan to develop its possibilities.

Isabella was named after her mother, Isabella of Portugal,

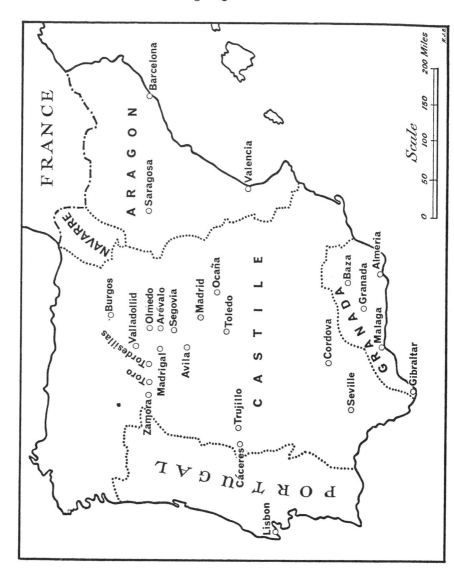

who was young, beautiful, intelligent and strong-willed. She had only recently married the King and though she soon contrived to get rid of his hated favourite, Don Alvaro, who had virtually controlled the government, she had not had time to make her own influence fully felt. King Juan died. His only son by his previous marriage took the crown as Enrique IV. The widowed Queen was at once pushed into the background. She had to retire to her castle at Arévalo, another of those bleak little towns in Avila, taking with her the three-year-old princess and a baby son, Alfonso.

It was a harsh country, fitting for young Isabella's hard upbringing. Life was plain and simple. The Queen was not rich. Her stepson had no love for her. There was no reason why anyone should make the troublesome journey to Arévalo to show friendliness or ask favours. The girl was taught mainly by local nuns, with occasional help from priests and tutors from the city of Avila, thirty miles away. Because of her rank she could not play with the town children. Her only friend was the castellan's daughter, Beatriz de Bobadilla, a tall dark girl of about the same age. Two occupations Isabella loved: all kinds of needlework, embroidery and weaving, that passed the endless hours in the solitary castle, and riding her horse over the tawny plateau, drinking in the sharp air and feasting her eyes upon the blue illimitable horizons of central Spain.

This life ended abruptly when she was about eleven. A summons came from her half-brother. In future she and little Alfonso were to live at court, in Segovia or Madrid or wherever it happened to be. So the children joined Enrique, and their mother was left alone in Arévalo, where she sank into an increasing depression and finally went out of her mind. Beatriz went to court with them. She was Isabella's closest friend for life.

73

The country-bred children stepped into a new world which, behind its outer seeming of splendid robes and shining armour, stately dances and tremulous fanfares, was essentially ugly and disordered. Alfonso was too young to grasp its nature. The girls were perhaps more sensitive to the undercurrents of personal relationship around them, more instinctively on guard against evils they could not always name.

Enrique was now turned thirty, a degenerate shiftless individual with a beautiful but unfaithful wife, a handsome but disloyal favourite, Don Beltrán de la Cueva, who carried on a love affair with that wife behind his back, and a new-born daughter Juana, whom he never knew for certain to be his own. No one, indeed, knew or will ever know who Juana's father was. Enrique's cynical and contemptuous courtiers gave her the nickname La Beltraneja. It was perhaps the nagging doubt, was she of the royal blood or not, that caused the King to send for his half-brother and half-sister at this time. For, if Juana was not rightful heir to his throne, Alfonso was, and after him, Isabella. It was safest to have them all under his eye.

In that corrupt, immoral court the King could trust nobody. Not the Queen, certainly. Nor his supposed friend, Don Beltrán. Nor the great lords who were jealous of Don Beltrán, outstanding among them the former favourite, Enrique's one-time tutor, the ambitious Marquess of Villena, and his blustering uncle, the fighting Archbishop of Toledo. Plotting and intrigue went on continually. Rebellious groups formed and reformed in secret. There was just one element the King could depend upon: his bodyguard. They were swarthy, turbanned Moors from the South, oddly out of place round the throne of a Catholic monarch whose forefathers had battled so often to drive the infidel out of Spain. But it was not so odd in fact. They were hated by all but the King who paid them. If anything happened to Enrique, they were lost. So they guarded him well.

Even a young girl could see that something was rotten in the kingdom. Petitions flowed in from decent folk who had suffered violence and injustice: the King ignored them. Lanky, with ponderous lolling head and broken nose, he sat moodily in one of his castles or went hunting in his forests, delighting in the blood and death of animals. To his subjects he was a byword, a bad joke. Isabella saw that her half-brother was scarcely half a man, and certainly not half a king.

Civil war seemed likely to break out at any moment. A host of Castilian grandees gathered in Burgos and issued an ultimatum: the King must reform his habits, dismiss Don Beltrán, and recognize Alfonso as his rightful heir, not the new-born Juana, 'La Beltraneja', who, said the rebels bluntly, 'is quite obviously not Your Highness's daughter'.

At first the frightened King agreed to everything. He sent away Don Beltrán and transferred his chief honours to Isabella's brother, whom he gave into the charge of Villena. Isabella, so recently snatched from her mother's care, now found herself parted from Alfonso as well. She had to stay with Enrique and his loose-living queen, and be godmother to the child Juana whose arrival had touched off the trouble. She had only Beatriz to confide in.

Soon Enrique broke all his promises. Don Beltrán was brought back, raised to a dukedom, endowed with fresh estates. Again the rebel grandees mustered their armies. The moving spirit was the Archbishop of Toledo. 'Tell your King,' he ordered the royal messenger, 'I am sick of him and his doings. Now we shall see who is the true King of Castile.'

His nephews, the Marquess of Villena and Pedro Girón, were less staunch. They agreed to change sides, rejoining Enrique for a price. The price was that Isabella should marry Pedro. She was horrified when she heard, for Pedro's reputation was even worse than his brother's. Beatriz is said to have snatched up a dagger and threatened to kill him. But the situation never came to a crisis: at the eleventh hour Pedro fell suddenly ill and died.

Meantime the civil war came to a head. The rebels proclaimed Alfonso their rightful king. The armies moved to meet each other. The royal ladies waited anxiously for the result behind the high walls of Segovia, in a citadel of fairy-tale splendour, all alabaster and arabesques, with silver walls and golden ceilings like giant honeycomb.

The armies clashed at Olmedo. The battle raged for three hours, the boy Alfonso nominally leading his men but the belligerent Archbishop (wearing mail under his red cloak) in actual control, and even Enrique taking the field on the opposite side, though he soon withdrew when the blood began to flow.

Who had won? Rumours and reports poured into Segovia. It was impossible—it is still impossible—to say who had had the best of it. But, having made sure that both the rival kings were still alive, the commander in Segovia decided to back Alfonso, and word was sent, inviting him to take possession of the city. Isabella took a chance too. She withdrew from the Queen's company and waited in another part of the palace with Beatriz for her brother to arrive.

It was the end of the summer, 1467. There would be no more serious fighting until next year: medieval armies could not be kept together for winter campaigns, least of all amid the bleak uplands of Spain. So, when Alfonso came, he and Isabella did the obvious thing. They went home to Arévalo, celebrated Alfonso's fourteenth birthday and then Christmas soon afterwards, and tried to rouse their mother from the mental strangeness into which she was falling.

What would the new year bring? Final victory? Alfonso unchallenged king? Isabella wondered what it would be like as elder sister to a boy king. Or would the civil war drag on endlessly, like the terrible struggle in England between their remote cousins of Lancaster and their even remoter cousins of York?

It was pestilence that the new year brought to Arévalo. Alfonso's life was precious. As the hot summer drew nearer, his followers insisted on their leaving. But fate seemed against them. At a wayside halt near Avila Alfonso was suddenly taken ill, and by the next morning he was dead. Some spoke of plague, others blamed the trout he had eaten for supper, others again murmured of poison. Isabella made them take his body back to Arévalo, the only place they had ever thought of as home. Then she rode to Avila and asked shelter, for the time being, in a convent in the city.

She needed a breathing space. A space to mourn and pray and be comforted, for she was a devout girl. And a space to think and face her new problems, for she had to live in this world before passing to the next. She cared about the tragic condition of Castile, and she never forgot that she was a king's daughter, with the responsibilities of her royal blood.

In the convent she could stave off the hard-faced scheming men who had turned from her brother's grave and crowded round her, pressing her to take over the leadership against Enrique and let them proclaim her Queen of Castile. It was not that she shrank from the crown: surely anyone could make a better job of government than this perverted neurotic who had let his country slide into anarchy? Few seventeen-year-olds in her place would have resisted the temptation, but Isabella's commonsense warned her it would be a dangerous gamble. When at last she gave her answer to the Archbishop and his allies she disappointed them.

'Restore the kingdom to my brother, Don Enrique,' she bade them, 'and in this way you will bring back peace to Castile.' But she added a shrewd condition: Enrique must solemnly name her as his successor and this must be endorsed by the Cortes, the assembly of noblemen and bishops corresponding to the medieval Parliament. Enrique was twenty-six years older than Isabella, he had already disowned Juana and cut her out of the succession, and it was unlikely that he would ever have, or claim to have, any other child. Isabella could afford to wait her turn.

Enrique, no fighting man, seemed delighted with the settlement. But it was not long before, under the pressure of his party, he began to wriggle out of all his promises.

The simplest way to deal with this tiresome young half-sister was to marry her to some foreign royalty and so get her out of Castile. He revived an old scheme to make her the second wife of his own brother-in-law, the Portuguese King Alfonso V, known as 'El Africano' because of his exploits against the Moors. Isabella had no intention of agreeing. The widower was fat and old enough to be her father, and they were too nearly related already. Besides, Enrique had promised never to force her into a marriage she disliked.

Yet he was planning to do just that. He thought of clapping her into the Alcazar, or fortified palace, at Madrid. But Isabella was too popular with the citizens of Ocaña, where the court then was, and he dared not anger them. In a huff he departed to Andalusia, leaving spies to report on her doings.

While Enrique was away, a French cardinal brought her an alternative proposal: would she marry the Duke of Berri, brother and heir to King Louis XI of France? Isabella could not refuse outright. She had to play for time, make polite excuses . . . princesses could not speak their minds bluntly like peasant lasses. She received a confidential report on the Duke's appearance. He was spindly-legged and bleary-eyed, and he sounded as odd as Enrique himself.

Isabella had to keep her enemies guessing while she strove desperately to bring off a counter-plan of her own, one favoured by her staunch supporter, the Archbishop of Toledo, and implacably opposed by Enrique.

This was to marry her cousin Ferdinand, if the Pope would allow it. Unlike all the other bridegrooms suggested for her, Ferdinand was of her own generation, actually almost a year younger. Further, though she had never met him, she knew him to be presentable, indeed rather dashing, and beloved by the Aragonese. Brown-eyed, black-haired, and swarthy, he was her opposite, a foil to her fairness. And in another, far more significant way, each had what the other had not, for he was heir to his father, the King of Aragon, and one day Castile would be hers, and if those kingdoms were joined nearly all Spaniards would be united under one crown.

Ferdinand sounded willing enough, but communication was difficult. It was not the easiest matter for a boy and girl to discuss direct when they had never seen each other. They were still separated by many miles of mountainous country and Enrique's spies were watching to intercept messengers. Though the King was still away in the south, he was keeping a keen eye on his half-sister. His patience was ebbing as she continued to find excuses to avoid the Portuguese marriage.

At Ocaña she felt like a prisoner. She found a pretext to move north to Avila. She might have joined her mother in the castle at Arévalo, but Enrique chose that moment to give it to one of his favourites. Isabella's poor mother, now quite unbalanced, was turned out of her own property. She went to Madrigal, and Isabella followed her there. It was not a very safe resting-place but it was another move northwards, away from Enrique.

Not a moment too soon, and not far enough. Things began to happen more rapidly. Knowing that her time was running out, Isabella sent a courier to Ferdinand in the Aragonese capital, Saragossa. She made her meaning plain. She was ready to marry him at once. Was *he* ready to come to her?

It was an awkward moment, the youth replied, there was revolt in Catalonia and trouble with the French. His father, now nearly blind, could not spare him at such a time. No sooner had Isabella received this news than she heard even worse. Enrique had ordered her arrest. In three days his soldiers would be clattering through the gates of Madrigal.

She had one friend she could turn to, the Archbishop of Toledo, who had never been happy about the settlement with Enrique. She sent word of her peril. The warrior churchman did not hesitate. He gathered three hundred horsemen and rode hell for leather to Madrigal, gathering another two hundred cavaliers on the way. They won the race against the King's troops. Then, without wasting time, they continued northwards, taking Isabella and her attendants with them. Only when they reached the strong walled city of Valladolid, where the people were in favour of Isabella and her marriage to Ferdinand, did the Archbishop feel that they could safely halt.

Isabella now sent two emissaries to Aragon, one her own chamberlain, to impress upon Ferdinand the absolute urgency of the situation. She could do no more. Apart from pride, she could not herself go to Aragon, for Enrique's troops held all the country between. But if Ferdinand wanted her, and if he was a man, as she believed he was, it was for him to find a way.

September passed—no certain news. Then, in the first week of October, her emissaries returned. All was well. The prince—no, the 'King of Sicily', for his father had just given him that title to increase his status for the wedding— was on his way. But he was coming neither as prince nor as king; he was disguised as a mule-driver, with a string of pack-mules and half a dozen noble companions no less ragged and filthy. They were travelling under cover of darkness and using lonely tracks across the mountains. It was their only hope of slipping through the cordon of Enrique's men.

Would they succeed? There were a few more days of anxiety. Then word came: Ferdinand had arrived safely at Burgo de Osma, another Castilian town that had little love for Enrique. An escort of cavaliers galloped off to welcome him, and on October 14, 1469, after dark had fallen, the young man knocked at the postern gate of Valladolid. He was let in by the Archbishop, who stood waiting in the torchlight. They crossed an orchard to the house where Isabella was staying. There the plighted couple met for the first time in their lives. They talked until two o'clock in the morning. Four days later, in that same house, their marriage was solemnized, and, though it was no state wedding with pomp and pageantry, the delighted townsfolk plunged into a week of festivities.

The historic partnership of Ferdinand and Isabella was formed. Even their warmest supporters could scarcely have prophesied all that it would mean to Spain.

What would Enrique do?

For a long time the angry King kept them in suspense. In vain Isabella wrote and sent her representatives to explain her actions and seek peace. Enrique sent cold and non-committal answers. He neither forgave her nor used force to show who was master.

She dared not leave Castile. If she fled with her bridegroom, she could say goodbye to her inheritance. Nor would Aragon welcome her as a landless exile. Not everyone there favoured the marriage. To those who did, it seemed desirable as the union of two kingdoms, not two young people. If Ferdinand and Isabella were to justify their act to their supporters, never mind their enemies, they must somehow hold their perilous ground in Castile.

The lovers moved to a castle twenty miles away at Dueñas, where they were safer. It is fair to call them 'lovers'. They had met as strangers, but they were warm-blooded, good-looking young people, anxious to like each other, bound up in a common adventure, a common dream. Either, or both, could have been disappointed and shied away. It was more likely and natural that they would fall into each other's arms, and that was what happened. The marriage turned out far better than most. Isabella, for all her strong and independent character, made a devoted wife. Ferdinand, who was never a saint, who had had love affairs before and was to have others in the future, was loyal to the essence of their partnership.

They agreed that, in their delicate political situation, they must never fall out, never let cunning enemies play them off one against the other. Even in the heat of first love, they were cool-headed enough—or certainly Isabella was— to see the importance of putting things down in black and white. She did not go to the altar until Ferdinand had signed a document making a series of promises about the future government of Castile. When she came to the throne, he would share (as her husband) in some of her authority, though certain privileges would remain hers alone. She was not giving up any of her rights, merely taking him into partnership, and junior partnership so far as Castile was concerned. If Ferdinand had objected to this, she could have pointed out that it was not for her own sake: her supporters would never have accepted a master brought in from Aragon.

For a whole uneasy year they waited to see what Enrique would do. They were short of money. They could hardly pay their bodyguard, and in fifteenth-century Europe that was the most dangerous economy to make. Isabella was going to have a baby. No sooner had she given birth, to a girl who was baptized Isabella, than shattering news arrived.

Enrique had gone back on his former decision. He had announced that after all the eight-year-old Princess Juana was his own daughter and the lawful heiress to his crown. He had made sure of French support by betrothing her to King Louis' brother, that same duke whom Isabella had avoided marrying.

All was not lost, however. It was one thing for the King to make a ruling, quite another to enforce it. Castile remained the lawless country it had been throughout his reign. Great nobles and bishops simply ignored the King's wishes if it suited them. Cities and regions made no secret of their loyalty to Isabella. The Cortes, though twice summoned, refused to swear allegiance to Juana. A strong-willed king could soon have had a civil war on his hands. As it was, Enrique did not push matters. Things trembled on the brink of violence but the swords remained sheathed. It was lucky, because in 1472 the French King's brother died mysteriously (after dining with Louis, who never much liked him) and this part of Enrique's plan fell to the ground.

Alternative schemes to provide Juana with a husband did not make much progress. There seemed a fair chance that Enrique would veer round once more and name Isabella his heiress. Beatriz was in a good position to help, for she too was now married, and her husband, Andrés de Cabrera, was Enrique's chamberlain. They worked on the King. Just before Christmas, 1473, Beatriz herself brought the good news to Isabella: Enrique was ready for a reconciliation at Segovia.

Could he be trusted? Isabella was not frightened but she took sensible precautions. She asked Ferdinand to remain for the time being outside Segovia, ready for emergencies. She then set out for the meeting, arriving at the height of the Christmas festivities. Everything went splendidly. Her odd half-brother showed charm and consideration. He sang for her and she danced. In the New Year's Eve procession he went on foot holding her horse's bridle. The next morning, all fear removed, Ferdinand joined the party.

Enrique, for all his amiability, could not be brought to the point, the official reinstatement of Isabella as his successor. She had powerful enemies: especially Villena, who had changed his title (he was now 'Master of Santiago') but not his position as the King's evil genius. He had been away during the Christmas festivities. He hurried back, sowing suspicions, unsuccessfully urging the arrest of Isabella and Ferdinand, but managing at least to cast a blight on the proceedings. Soon he persuaded the King to ride off with him into the westerly region of Extremadura.

Isabella and Ferdinand remained in Segovia. They felt safe enough. The city favoured Isabella, and with friends at court like Beatriz and her husband they were protected against sudden treachery. They felt so secure that by the late summer Ferdinand left Isabella to visit his father in Aragon. In his absence things happened quickly.

Early in October Isabella received news that the Master
of Santiago was dead. She might cross herself and murmur
a charitable prayer for the repose of his soul, but she could
not help sleeping more soundly in the knowledge that her
most implacable adversary was gone. Two months later
came another galloping courier, from Madrid, forty-five
miles away. Enrique, ailing since the beginning of the year,
had collapsed suddenly and died in great agony.

That night there was no sleep for Isabella or for anyone
in the palace at Segovia.

There was not a moment to lose. She could not wait for
Ferdinand to come back. She must be crowned Queen of
Castile first thing in the morning, with whatever ceremonial
could be put on at such short notice. How fortunate that
this had happened when she was at Segovia, and that the
crown jewels were there to lend an authentic dignity to the
occasion!

There was good reason for this haste. Enrique had never
confirmed her succession to the throne. Her enemies might
try to crown Juana. The child had been left in the custody
of the new Marquess of Villena, son of Enrique's crony and
just as much Isabella's enemy. He might use her as a
figure-head for the opposition party.

So, on December 13, 1474, after a night of prayer and
feverish practical arranging, the twenty-three-year-old
Isabella rode in procession through the streets of Segovia
and was solemnly enthroned on a hastily erected platform
in the great square. When Ferdinand arrived home he was
vexed at having been left out, and she had to use all her
tact to smooth things over and make him see how vital it
had been to act at once. Ferdinand's sensitiveness was
understandable. *She* was now a sovereign in her own right,

*he* had still to inherit Aragon, where his father, though blind and old, seemed unlikely to lay down the sceptre in the near future. It was not easy in those days for a man to play second fiddle to his wife.

Soon enough he saw that Isabella had not exaggerated the danger. Villena did form a party to back Juana's claim, and to Isabella's consternation he was joined by her oldest and most influential supporter, the Archbishop of Toledo. The reason for this was hard to see, except that the Archbishop was a born meddler and insatiably ambitious. His influence over Isabella was sure to wane as her strong character matured and she felt the reins of power in her grasp. A young girl like Juana, weak, dependent, a pawn to be moved by her backers, now offered him more scope.

Much worse was to come. Whoever had been Juana's father, there was no doubt that the King of Portugal was her uncle, that same Alfonso 'El Africano' whom Isabella had refused to marry. Now Alfonso not merely backed Juana's claim to Castile but announced that he intended to marry her. That he was already her uncle was a difficulty the Pope could remove. That he was even older and fatter than when Isabella had turned him down, and the age-gap between him and Juana even wider, was a circumstance even the Pope could not alter, but one that troubled no one in that period of political marriages, except perhaps the unlucky princess herself.

Old and fat the King of Portugal might be, but he was a formidable soldier, and when he rode into the north-western corner of her realm at the head of twenty thousand men, Isabella felt a sinking of the heart. She and Ferdinand could not, at that moment, count on more than a few hundred.

Perhaps it was well that the odds were so hopelessly against them. It made Alfonso over-confident. He wasted weeks on leisurely formalities, waiting to collect Juana, to go through a betrothal ceremony, to have them proclaimed King and Queen of Castile, and then to celebrate at leisure in (bitter irony for Isabella) her girlhood home of Arévalo.

Meanwhile, from May to early July, Ferdinand and Isabella worked feverishly to create an army out of nothing. He rode one way, she donned armour and rode another, galloping from castle to castle, city to city, rousing her people. She was expecting another child. Because of that supreme exertion she never bore it. It was just part of the price she was to pay throughout her life for being a queen.

Between them they mustered a motley, ill-equipped, untrained host double the size of Alfonso's, but they could not bring the Portuguese King to battle. They could not find food for such a multitude and had to retreat with nothing accomplished. Still Alfonso did not strike, thinking no doubt that their forces would melt away as the months went by. Not so. Ferdinand and Isabella used the autumn and winter to put their army into proper shape. They weeded out the useless and brought the numbers down to fifteen thousand. They raised some money from the cities and much from the Church: Isabella, a devout daughter of the Church if ever there was one, requisitioned half its immense treasure of silver with the promise, faithfully kept, that it would be repaid within three years. Lack of cannon had been a serious weakness. Now, with ample funds, they could buy the best from Italy and Germany. At the end of that year, 1475, they took the field again, Ferdinand leading the main force while Isabella commanded a separate army of horsemen in the rear.

Two months passed in manoeuvres round Zamora on the Duero. Then, towards sunset on March 1, the Portuguese turned at bay near Toro, higher up the river, and in an hour or two of bloody fighting the issue was settled.

87

Isabella was encamped at Tordesillas, not far away. She was awakened with the news of victory. Ferdinand was safe and triumphant, the Portuguese had fought well but were now in utter rout. Castile was safe.

Isabella ordered a thanksgiving service and went barefoot to church.

Some rebellious cities remained, some great noblemen of doubtful loyalty, but Isabella was now the unchallenged Queen of Castile. The Archbishop of Toledo had to bow his stiff neck and beg forgiveness. Dividing their forces as before, Ferdinand took the northern provinces and she the south. Patiently and diplomatically she established her authority. She wished to bring peace, not the sword. The cities of Trujillo and Cáceres opened their gates; the Andalusian grandees, the Duke of Medina Sidonia and the Marquess of Cadiz, were won over by her charm. She worked hard for these bloodless victories, but, as she told her anxious councillors, 'Sovereigns who wish to rule well cannot avoid their duties.'

Juana La Beltraneja was never again used as a puppet queen against her. The hapless girl became a nun in Portugal. From time to time proposals cropped up that she should marry this prince or that (with the necessary release from her vows that royalty could usually obtain) but nothing came of them, and she always returned to the cloisters in the end.

From the moment of her coronation Isabella had been dedicated to the task she had dreamed of since, as a girl of strict standards and sincere religion, she had had to witness the immorality of Enrique's court. From the first she had resolved to stop such scandals and set a different tone. Now that she was fully mistress of her kingdom, she could be bolder.

This was the period in which other monarchs were breaking the power of their barons. In England, notably, Henry VII did so after his victory at Bosworth in 1485. Isabella started some years earlier, but by gentler means. The grandees were induced to give up some of their privileges. They were quietly deprived of others by law. Isabella became an energetic law-maker: the laws of the country were in a mighty tangle, dating back centuries, and she often preferred to cut away the tangle and spin a simpler web of her own. In the process she strengthened the position of the Crown.

She meant her laws to be obeyed. Castile had been an unruly country, with brigands infesting the roads and robber-barons taking toll of harmless travellers from their castles. She stopped that. Scores of petty castles were pulled down. She organized a corps of mounted police, the Santa Hermandad or 'Holy Brotherhood', who dealt vigorously with the brigands.

She was no tyrant, but the trend of the century made her an autocrat, an almost all-powerful personal ruler. Like Elizabeth of England, a hundred years later, she warmly loved her subjects and spoke of them as her 'children'. The Cortes, like the English Parliament, was called together mainly to vote money. Isabella could not be expected to practise democracy, for she had never heard of it, but she listened to advice and tried to do what seemed best for her people. Her regulations for trade and agriculture might not always prove wise in the long run—she knew no more of economics than of democracy—but she restored the value of the debased currency and rescued her country from the extravagance of its previous rulers.

Perhaps her greatest mistake was to admit the Holy Inquisition into Spain.

Long ago, in 1233, a Pope had established this body to

put down heretics. It operated only in some countries. It never reached England, and only in 1480 did Isabella, under pressure, admit it to Castile. Ferdinand, who had at last succeeded his father in 1479, did not let the inquisitors begin their trials, torturings and burnings in Aragon until 1487.

The Spanish Inquisition was not, at this period, dealing with 'Protestant' heretics. Martin Luther was barely out of his cradle in far-away Germany, and both Ferdinand and Isabella were dead before he nailed his famous defiance to the church door. The Spanish Inquisition was not concerned with Catholic thinkers who clashed with official Church teaching. But many of Ferdinand and Isabella's subjects were Jews or Moors, two peoples who had played a great part in the building up of Spanish civilization, and for centuries had been loyal subjects of the Christian kings. Some had remained Jewish or Moslem in religion, others had adopted Christianity. Human nature being what it is, many converts had been influenced by hopes of personal advantage or fears of unpopularity rather than by genuine religious conviction. It was mainly against these luke-warm believers that the Inquisition launched its campaign.

From the start the religious issue became muddled with racial intolerance. Once, it had been possible for all peoples and creeds to exist side by side in a Spanish city; Christians, Jews, Moslem Moors, converts and non-converts alike. Now, under 'the Catholic Sovereigns', as Ferdinand and Isabella were jointly referred to, the idea developed that the whole nation must be unified in faith. In 1492, a memorable year for other reasons, the Jews were expelled. Ten years later it was the turn of the Moors. Apart from the suffering inflicted on this multitude of refugees themselves, much damage was done to the prosperity of Spain through the loss of so many productive and talented inhabitants.

It is fair to remember (though it does not fully excuse their intolerance) that for the ten years *before* 1492 Ferdinand and Isabella were fighting a bitter war against the Moorish kingdom of Granada. Not only might their own Moorish subjects be suspected of a sneaking sympathy with the enemy, but their Jewish subjects also, for in past centuries the Spanish Jews had usually found the Moslems kinder and more broad-minded than the Christians.

This war was provoked by Isabella and Ferdinand, the crowning stage in their master-plan, dreamed of since their marriage and their first determination to unite the whole peninsula.

First they had secured Castile and put that weakened realm in good order. Then Ferdinand had inherited Aragon. With luck Portugal would eventually come into the family by marriage: their little daughter, Isabella, was betrothed to Prince Alfonso, their old enemy's grandson. They could do nothing more about Portugal. And they dared not touch Navarre, straddling the Pyrenees, too close to France. But Granada, proud remnant of a dazzling epoch when Moorish civilization had covered Spain—Granada, with its lovely cities and its lush plain a pattern of orchards watered by the Sierra Nevada snows, was like an immense golden orange ripe for their basket.

Isabella was as eager for the struggle as her soldier husband. From childhood, like every Spaniard, she had fed her imagination on songs and stories of the age-old vendetta with the Moors. Both as patriot and as Christian she longed to sweep them into the sea. The war would be a holy crusade.

The ten-year struggle had many ups and downs. The Moors had long ago lost the dash that had once carried them in triumph to the Pyrenees. They were weakly ruled and divided by quarrels. They avoided open battles when they could, but were cunning in ambushes and guerrilla tactics, so that the Christians suffered some grave catastrophes. Once, in the ravines near Loja, Ferdinand himself was beset by the enemy and saved only by the courage of the Marquess of Cadiz.

Isabella took part in these campaigns, using her remarkable gifts as an organizer. Men, money, food, fodder, arms, horses, tents, gunpowder: all must be in the right place at the right time. Few armies in bygone centuries were efficiently served with supplies. Perhaps Isabella, as a woman, instinctively grasped their importance, but the main thing was that she had a clear intelligence, a command of detail, and a physical toughness that enabled her to ride thousands of miles over rough mountain trails, ensuring that everything was done.

Her headquarters, wherever they were, became her home. The children went with her, accompanied by their nurses and teachers. She meant them to have a more thorough education than she had herself received from the sketchily qualified nuns of Arévalo.

When the war began, the eldest, Isabella, was eleven, Juan three, Juana two. Others were born amid the stresses of campaigning. Maria arrived in 1482 (her twin was born dead) and three years later came Catherine, that ill-fated Catherine of Aragon whose marriage to Henry VIII was to have such far-reaching results in English history.

Isabella was tragically unfortunate in her family. The first two children were to die young, in her own lifetime. Juana, who was to succeed her as Queen of Castile, became a neurotic, was inhumanly ill-treated after her mother's death, and is labelled in the records, rather unfairly, as Juana la Loca—'Joan the Mad'. Maria alone attained happiness as wife of King Manuel the Great of Portugal.

As the war dragged on, Isabella became even more active.

She appeared in the fighting zone, clad in armour, riding along the lines of her army, stirring them to fresh efforts. Her spirit braced the wavering. When the siege of Baza seemed hopeless, it was she who insisted that it must go on, pawning her crown to raise money and riding across the snow-covered hills to see the situation herself. Within three days the Moors decided to surrender.

Now the tide was flowing steadily towards victory. Town after town, castle after castle, fell to the Spaniards —or rather to the crusading army that Isabella's idealism had gathered under her banner, for there were soldiers drawn from all parts of Christendom: Germans, Poles, Swiss, French and Irish, not to mention a contingent of the fearsome English bowmen.

In the spring of 1491 the two sovereigns began the long siege of the Moorish capital, Granada of the red towers, rising from the plain on its precipitous hills, crowned with the exquisite gardens, terraces, courts and fountains of the Alhambra, and backed with the glistening whiteness of the Sierra Nevada. Boabdil, last of the Moorish kings, knew that defeat was only a matter of time. On the second day of 1492 he rode sadly out and handed his keys to Ferdinand, who passed them over to Isabella.

Their life-long dream was fulfilled. Granada was theirs, Spain was united, everywhere the Faith was triumphant.

Among those watching the unforgettable scene, that January day, was the Genoese navigator, Christopher Columbus. For five or six years he had been trying to win royal support for an expedition to test his theory that India could be reached by sailing westwards across the unknown Atlantic. The Kings of Portugal and England had already refused him. Isabella and Ferdinand had postponed a final decision, fobbing him off with committees and inquiries, saying truthfully enough that they were too much absorbed in their Moorish war to go into his scheme.

Now he lost no time in reminding them of his existence. Isabella agreed to receive him. In the domed audience-chamber of the Alhambra she listened to his eloquent theories and sweeping demands. The latter were too much for her. He insisted on being made an admiral at once and viceroy of all the lands he might discover, with ten per cent of any gold and silver found there. Isabella shook her head. Columbus rode away. He had finished with these Spaniards. Perhaps the French would have more imagination?

In the nick of time Isabella was persuaded to change her mind. Beatriz, still constantly at her side, was one of those who urged her. A messenger hastened after Columbus and overtook him ten miles along the road. The rest belongs to world history. Columbus sailed in the following August, sighted his first West Indian island in October, and by March, 1493, was back in Spain, entertaining Isabella and Ferdinand with the story of his first voyage. By May the Pope had proclaimed them the rightful owners of all lands, known or unknown, west of a line drawn down the middle of the Atlantic. Without yet realizing it, Isabella had collected for her heirs an American empire stretching from California to Cape Horn.

She never knew its extent, let alone suspected the consequences, both glorious and terrible, of unveiling the New World to the Old. The Spanish Conquest, with all its atrocities, had not begun when, on November 26, 1504, she died at Medina del Campo, not far from Madrigal of the High Towers where she had first seen the light of day fifty-three years before. She was not buried there, nor at near-by Arévalo. Instead, and fittingly, her coffin was carried south to Granada, the city she had striven so long to win. Her tomb and her kneeling effigy may still be seen there in the royal chapel of the cathedral, but it might well be said that the whole of Spain is her monument.


## THE YEARS BETWEEN 1504–1626

Isabella had united Spain. Spain, under her successors, went on to conquer the new world revealed by Columbus, and also to become the greatest power in Europe. The century following Isabella's death is Spain's century. It was the age of the Conquistadores in Mexico and Peru, of the matchless Spanish pikemen triumphant in Europe from Italy to the Netherlands, and of the 'Invincible Armada' sent against England—one of the ventures that failed.

By the beginning of the next century the balance of power was changing. Spain had exhausted her effort and was slipping into a long period of decline and decay. France was rising after a spell of weakness and civil wars. Her great age was approaching, under the 'Sun King', Louis XIV. But it had not quite arrived. Between the heyday of Spain and the heyday of France comes an interlude when, perhaps surprisingly, the spotlight of history shifts to Sweden.

Surprisingly, because today Sweden is thought of as a small nation, devoted to peace and progress, anxious only to remain neutral in the quarrels of the great powers. But in this period, when all Europe was split by the Reformation, with Catholics and Protestants everywhere in murderous conflict, Sweden's soldier king, Gustavus Adolphus, made himself champion of the Protestants.

Earlier, in Isabella's day, there had been no separate Swedish kingdom. With Norway, the country had been united under the Danish crown. Then in 1523 the Swedes had declared their independence under one of their own noblemen, Gustavus Vasa. His descendants ruled with varying success, but Sweden remained a poorish, backward country of lakes and forests, without great advantages, until Gustavus Adolphus inherited the crown when he was only seventeen. That was 1611. Shakespeare was writing his last plays in London. It would be another nine years before the Pilgrim Fathers set out in the *Mayflower*.

It was not so long before Gustavus Adolphus proved his prowess as 'the Lion of the North'. An inspired and inspiring cavalry general, he defeated both the Poles and the Russians, stripping them of their territories until he almost turned the Baltic into a Swedish lake. Many young English gentlemen, serving as volunteers with him, learned the tactics they were later to use in the headlong charges of their own Civil War. In such charges there was always danger for the King. Gustavus Adolphus never flinched from such danger, but he could not help fearing for the future of his country if he were killed. In 1626 he was thirty-two, had been married six years, but had no heir. He was therefore filled with hope and anxiety as the year moved to its end and the birth of the Queen's child drew near.

# 5. Christina of Sweden

Clearly the new baby would be a boy, the Crown Prince that Sweden needed to carry on the greatness the country was assuming in the affairs of Europe. Everyone in the palace at Stockholm was agreed on that point as the year 1626 drew to its dark close.

It was not just that the King so passionately desired a son, or that the Queen (dull, unpopular German princess though she was) deserved one to make up for the two other children she had already borne and lost. The Court astrologers forecast, and practically guaranteed, a boy. All the signs were right. Accordingly, all the preparations were made to celebrate the arrival of a future king.

A week or two before Christmas the baby was born. The women barely glanced at the hairy, ugly little thing before rushing off through the palace to spread the expected good news. Too late it was realized that they had jumped to a false conclusion. Princesses too, when newly born, can be ugly little things. The Court ladies had vied with each other in their keenness to tell the King that he had a son. There was no competition now to inform him that he had a daughter instead.

Their anguished debate was ended when the King's half-sister, Princess Catherine, volunteered to break the news to him. She was a tactful woman, but she soon found that she need not have wasted time beating about the bush.

'Let us thank God, my sister,' said Gustavus Adolphus at once. 'I hope that this girl will fully make up to me for a son.' And he ordered that the solemn singing of a *Te Deum* and all the other rejoicings should go ahead exactly as planned.

It is evident now that this famous incident had a far-reaching significance and was much more than a tragicomical muddle caused by excited ladies-in-waiting.

In some senses perhaps—apart from what the kingdom of Sweden needed—Christina *should* have been a boy. Her tastes and mentality, as she grew up, were often to seem unnatural for a woman. True, she received a masculine kind of education, but so have many girls without their turning out any less feminine. Christina's odd career cannot be explained by her circumstances and upbringing alone. In her century it was not realized (as modern science has revealed) that no individual is born with one hundred per cent masculine characteristics or one hundred per cent feminine. Each is a blend combining some of both, usually with one type in so clear a majority that there is no hesitation in classifying that person as male or female, though it is common enough to speak of a 'mannish' woman or an 'effeminate' man. Much more rarely the sex characteristics are so evenly balanced that even physically, as well as psychologically, it becomes difficult to make the distinction. Had this problem been understood in Christina's time, she might have met with a good deal more sympathy.

The Queen had no more children. She disliked and resented Christina as a disappointment. The child sensed this from her earliest years. She turned to her father who (whatever his first pangs of regret) had so completely mastered his feelings that there was only the deepest affection between them. When she was two, she fell dangerously ill: Gustavus hastened back from a distant journey and, when she was better, ordered another *Te Deum* to be sung.

She idolized him as a hero, and well she might, for he was a hero to a great part of Europe—a dashing cavalier of a king, leading his armies to victory against Danes and Poles, Russians and Germans. Once, when he took her on a journey, it was suggested to him that the usual salute of guns should not be fired in his honour, lest the little girl be frightened. Gustavus shook his head. 'Let the salute be fired. She is a soldier's daughter.' And when the cannon duly roared, and some of the grown-up ladies went pale and covered their ears, Christina clapped her hands delightedly.

This king lived dangerously and knew it. When he sailed across the Baltic to conduct one of his campaigns, he was well aware that he might never return. He was a statesman as well as a soldier. The future of Sweden must be provided for. So, before departing as usual in 1630, he set up a Council of Regency to govern the country in his absence or, if he died, until Christina came of age at eighteen.

The King had no illusions about his wife. Queen Marie Eleonora was to have no say in the government or in the education of their child. Both matters were entrusted to the Prime Minister, a loyal friend and follower, Axel Oxenstierna, together with four other councillors, two of them members of the same Oxenstierna family that was dominant in Sweden. Christina was to be trained from her tenderest years to do the man's work that was her destiny. She must be guided neither by women nor by foreigners. And Marie Eleonora was both.

Of course no girl, even the cannon-loving Christina, could be expected to grow up without some feminine supervision. Gustavus (with some reason) decided that the best person to provide it was her aunt, that same Princess

Catherine who had handled matters so well on the day of her birth.

Before leaving for Germany, he took Christina—now three and a half—to a farewell ceremony and presented her to his subjects as his acknowledged heir. No one was to doubt that. In front of them all, he took her up in his arms and kissed her.

She cried for three days after he had gone. Two years passed. He was still away at the wars. She made such progress in her first lessons that she was able to send him little letters in the stiff, formal phrasing of the time.

She never saw him again. In 1632, a month before her sixth birthday, a battle was fought at Lützen in Saxony. It was a Swedish victory, but the King, charging with his cavalry through the fog, was mysteriously shot in the back. He was only thirty-eight. It would be twelve years before his daughter was old enough to mount the throne in his place.


After such a tragedy it was natural enough for a mother and child to draw together. Marie Eleonora now showed more interest in Christina than ever before. She took firm possession of her, and for the time being the Regency Council had too many urgent problems on their hands to argue with the royal widow.

There was, however, something more than natural— something morbid and repellent—about her behaviour.

She was entitled, if she wished, to parade her own grief by shutting herself up in a room hung with black velvet, with candles burning night and day, and with the embalmed heart of the King hanging over the bed in a golden case. It was another thing to make a healthy child share that room, and that whole way of life with her. Yet for two years this was Christina's fate, and lesson-time was almost her only escape. Is is not surprising that she became fond of study.

She was stifled and revolted by the sentimental, possessive displays of a mother she had never been at ease with. She was usually happier with men, anyhow.

When Axel Oxenstierna returned from Germany and was at last able to look into the matter, there was trouble.

Not only were the late King's wishes being ignored, he decided, but the Queen Mother's influence was upsetting the health and nerves of the future Queen.

Christina went off (as her father had decreed) to live with Princess Catherine, her husband, and their children. Furious, Marie Eleonora retired to a country castle at Gripsholm. Even her husband's heart was put back with the rest of his body, now brought home from Germany, and given a state burial. The ceremony, so long after her real loss, did not distress Christina too much. She had done her weeping. Life stretched ahead.

She made it a full life.

In mind and body alike she was tireless. Ten hours in the saddle, wearing a boy's breeches, or twelve hours bent over her books—indoors or out, it was all one to her. No horse daunted her: she grew into one of the finest riders in Sweden. As for study, she recalled in after years: 'I had an insatiable desire to know everything.' She boasted that she could manage with three hours' sleep.

She prided herself on her languages. She had learned to speak German with her mother from the first. She studied French: she was drawn to France as the centre of European elegance and learning, of which there was not too much in her own kingdom. In culture France had taken the place once held by Italy, just as in political power she was superseding Spain. That did not discourage Christina from learning Italian and Spanish too. European statesmen saw no need at that time to learn English. In any case, there was always Latin available as a common language between governments and scholars. Christina learnt Latin too and even Greek, revelling in the intellectual challenge of unseen translation and prose composition.

It is rather a relief to know that her French correspondence, still preserved, contains plenty of mistakes, and doubtless she was not as good at her other languages as she liked to think. But if she was not perfect she was certainly remarkable.

Mathematics appealed to her. She soon developed an interest in astronomy. She had also to apply her mind to theology. In the religious conflict bitterly dividing Europe, Christina was pledged to the path laid down by her father, champion of the Lutheran Protestant creed. From the first, though, she had an independent and critical attitude to everything.

Before she was eight, she had been taken to hear a long sermon on the Day of Judgment. Delivered in the eloquent hell-fire style of the period, with abundant gruesome detail, it had scared her out of her wits. Why hadn't she been warned before, she asked her favourite teacher, John Matthaie—would the Day of Judgment come tomorrow, and what would happen to her? Matthaie, a kindly man, reassured her as best he could without contradicting the official belief. A year later the theme of Judgment Day came up again in all its horror, for the service was a special annual event. This time she was unmoved. The following year she was openly scornful. Was the rest of religion, she demanded, no truer than the threatened Judgment Day that never arrived? The devoted Matthaie considered whipping her—it was the normal seventeenth-century recipe for driving the devil out of a child and winning it back to godliness—but Christina (if we can believe her own story) gave him such a look that he abandoned the idea. After that, though she had to appear in church and sit through endless sermons, she read or played with the dogs at her feet. She had not given up religion but she had privately turned away from her father's creed.

One subject she studied with the Prime Minister himself: politics, so vital to a ruler. Oxenstierna gave her long, almost daily sessions and was delighted with her quick grasp of matters not usually of interest to a child.

Unfortunately, to Oxenstierna and his fellow statesmen, politics meant chiefly wars, treaties and other foreign affairs. The Swedish government was not much concerned with the problems of the Swedish people, and Christina was not encouraged to develop that kind of concern herself.

In England, by this time, there was a big middle class demanding a say in its own destiny: though still far from modern democracy, the English were on the brink of the Civil War which cost their king his head and the Cavaliers their power. But in Sweden, and in Europe generally, government was still securely in the hands of the kings and their nobles, with little account taken of anyone else, a situation that went on until the French Revolution a hundred and fifty years later.

'You shall be made to realize,' Oxenstierna once bluntly told the dissatisfied peasants, 'that there are persons of high birth in this country!'

That was the arrogant spirit in which he educated his future sovereign. Arrogance, however, was a quality Christina had no need to cultivate. She had plenty.

Besides her studies and her riding, which included hunting, she learned to fence and dance. Purely feminine interests meant nothing to her. In clothes she preferred masculine styles, low shoes (though she was not tall), velvet caps like a cavalryman's, plain jackets, and skirts shorter and more practical than the voluminous garments of that century. Her clothes were often ink-spotted. She did not care.

'Some people,' she declared, 'are silly enough to be slaves to fashion. They are miserable if they do not spend their lives between mirror and comb. Tidiness is only for the idle.' She was never idle.

She was not without young company. Princess Catherine's daughters, Marie and Eleonora, shared some of her lessons, but not her enthusiasm for learning. She told their father he should make them work harder. It is hardly surprising that she was not invariably beloved by all.

She seemed more successful in her friendship with their brother, Charles Gustavus. He was four years older than Christina. In any case, she looked up to him as a boy. She had a low opinion of her own sex. Indeed, she was heard to say that no woman was fit to rule a country. This though she was preparing to rule one herself, and the memory of England's great Elizabeth was still green.

Princess Catherine died when Christina was eleven, but there was no question of returning the girl to her mother. She remained with her cousins. The Queen Mother departed without notice to Denmark—it is hardly true to say 'fled', because no one would have tried to stop her, but she went through the motions of a secret and melodramatic flight, and for many years never set foot in Sweden or saw her daughter again.

Christina meantime developed into a beautiful young woman, with big luminous eyes, fine hands and a perfect complexion. There was nothing boyish about her figure. Her masculinity was in her mind, and in the physical toughness, the capacity to endure hardship and fatigue, concealed behind her misleading exterior.

Such was the girl who reached her eighteenth birthday

in December, 1644, mounted a silver throne, and took the oath not as 'Queen' but as 'King' of Sweden. In England, that same year, King Charles had been beaten by Cromwell at Marston Moor and his crown was already in danger. There were no such movements of revolt in Sweden, and it was with her usual assurance that Christina entered at last into her delayed inheritance.

She had some idea of what she wanted. It was to end the long war in Germany that had started before she was born and had by now nearly earned the name history has given it, the Thirty Years' War. It had spread famine and ruin through Central Europe, so that those lands took generations to recover. It had not touched Swedish soil, but it had cost Sweden many lives, including her father's, and a crippling expense.

She wanted to stop that drain of blood and money. So far as the latter was concerned, she was not primarily interested in reducing taxes, still less in bettering the conditions of the common people. Seventeenth-century rulers seldom thought along those lines.

Christina took the simple view usual at the time. Subjects paid taxes: sovereigns spent the money as seemed best to them. The only people excused taxes were, oddly enough, the nobility, who had most money with which to pay. The nobility, however, had power too, and it took a bold king like Henry VII of England to challenge that power. Christina never tried. She had no wish to, though she was quite skilful at getting her own way by playing off one nobleman against another. She could out-manoeuvre even her old political teacher, Oxenstierna, when she had a mind to go against him.

She was, however, reasonably satisfied with the present system of government and taxation. What was unusual was the way in which she wanted to spend the money. It was to be lavished on the arts and sciences. She meant to educate and refine these rugged subjects of hers, to sharpen their wits and open their eyes to the elegances of life, to bring them the culture of France and Italy, to make Stockholm a modern Athens of the North.

It took her three years, and some unscrupulous contriving behind Oxenstierna's back, to end the war. The Treaty of Westphalia, in 1648, left Sweden in possession of wide lands on the eastern side of the Baltic, not only her old dominions in Finland and Karelia but what today is Soviet territory, stretching from the swamps where Leningrad now stands as far south as Riga.

Now Christina could develop her own ideas. Within twelve months she had scored her first triumph: she had induced the most famous philosopher alive, the Frenchman René Descartes, to come out of his seclusion in Holland and visit Stockholm. He took a lot of persuading. She had to send a ship to fetch him. But he was pleased with his reception. He wrote to his friend, the exiled Queen Elizabeth of Bohemia, that Christina's 'generosity and majesty . . . are

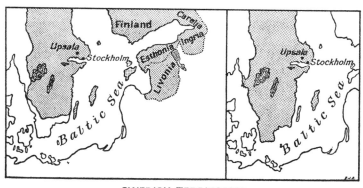

**SWEDISH TERRITORIES
IN 1648 —**      **AND TODAY**

106

combined with such sweetness and goodness as to make every one her willing slave. She is much given to study, though I cannot say what she will think of my philosophy, as she knows nothing of it yet.'

Christina was eager to remedy this gap in her knowledge. She insisted that he instruct her in a series of private sessions. It was unfortunate that her days were so full, but she could make time if he would come at five o'clock in the morning. This the unfortunate Descartes had to do. He must have wished that he had at least accepted quarters in the palace, instead of choosing to stay with his friend, Pierre Chanut, the French ambassador. He would have been spared the horrors of that riverside drive through the blackness of a mid-winter Scandinavian night. As it was, within a few months he died of inflammation of the lungs. Christina was widely blamed.

She was luckier in her other dealings.

Scholars, artists, craftsmen of all kinds, were drawn to her court as though to a magnet. Abroad, her agents bought up famous libraries of rare books and manuscripts. Shiploads of statuary, pictures, medallions and other art treasures were dispatched to Stockholm. Musicians, dancers and actors were invited from all over Europe to perform before her.

She herself took part in the elaborate masques then fashionable in the royal courts of Europe. These were spectacular entertainments combining splendid costumes and ingenious effects with music, dancing and tableaux, with the dramatic element reduced to a minimum. The themes were usually taken from classical mythology. In *The Death of Adonis,* Christina played a nymph, Arsinoë, and her beautiful maid-of-honour, Ebba Sparre, appeared as Venus. Her favourite courtier, the half-French Magnus de la Gardie, made a worthy Apollo in *The Gods' Banquet.*

Ebba Sparre and Magnus de la Gardie were her closest friends. She was devoted to the other girl. The masculine side of Christina's oddly mixed nature inspired her sometimes with an unduly passionate affection for persons of her own sex. On the other hand she was so intimate with the debonair Magnus that many people supposed them to be secret lovers. It seems unlikely. For all her powerful impulses and emotions, Christina seems to have been incapable of such a relationship.

Certainly she shrank from marriage, though her anxious councillors (like Elizabeth of England's) were continually urging it upon her for the safety of the state.

The obvious choice of bridegroom was her cousin, Charles Gustavus. They had grown up together, she admired him, and as a girl she had thought herself in love with him.

'*My love is so strong,*' she had written to him when she was seventeen, '*that it can only be overcome by death, and if, which God forbid, you should die before me, my heart shall be dead for anyone else . . .*'

However, the years passed, she mounted the throne, she was not only free to marry him but was being begged on all sides to do so, yet she avoided a decision. She knew more of life now and more of herself. She was repelled by the thought of married life, and above all by the prospect of bearing children.

In front of Magnus de la Gardie and her old tutor, Matthaie, she gave Charles Gustavus a plain hint not to be hopeful.

'I must tell you that I cannot promise to marry you at all. I can only promise that I will not marry anyone else. And,' she went on, 'I will promise you something more. Supposing that I decide never to marry, I will make you my successor to the throne.'

It was one thing to promise this to her cousin, it was

another to get it accepted by Oxenstierna and the Senate. It was debated in her presence, for, as was the custom, she presided at all meetings.

She had not yet been crowned. She wanted them to pass an Act of Succession, making her cousin her heir, but she refused to tell them yet what private undertaking she had given him.

'No one in the world can make me change the plan I have made. If I marry I shall marry no one but Charles Gustavus. But I will not tell you now if I shall marry. You will know after my coronation.'

Reluctantly the Senate passed the law. As Oxenstierna signed it, he remarked that he would have preferred to enter his grave instead. But Christina as usual had her way.

The actual coronation took place at the end of October, 1650, when she had been Queen for nearly six years. Previously, she withdrew from the city (staying with the de la Gardie family outside) so that she could make a processional entry, with her Guards marching in yellow and black uniforms, her blue-and-yellow-velvet pages, the senators and the foreign ambassadors in an endless column of ornate coaches, trumpeters, drummers, footmen, archers, halberdiers and the rest.

Prince Charles Gustavus had a special place there, and later stood beside her throne in the cathedral. But in the ordinary way he lived rather sulkily on his estates on the island of Öland, and took no prominent part in public life.

Almost at the end of the procession came Christina's mother, returning for the occasion after her years of absence abroad.

For a time Christina kept up the killing tempo of public work and private study she had set herself. She presided at

Senate meetings, conferred with her ministers, received ambassadors, conducted correspondence, founded learned institutions, talked with scholars, and took the lead in balls, masques and entertainments of every kind.

Once she was inspecting a new warship in the Stockholm dockyards at four o'clock in the morning—presumably on one of those northern midsummer mornings when the night is no more than a few hours of luminous twilight— and as she stood with her admiral on a narrow gangway over the water the man lost his balance and fell, taking her with him. An equerry dived in to the rescue. He grasped the Queen by the skirt, while at the same time the admiral, struggling blindly beneath the surface, clutched at her in his instinct to save himself. Between the two of them, and the encumbering petticoats she hated, Christina was nearly drowned. However, another man in the party managed to drag her free, and as soon as she recovered her breath and spat out the harbour-water, her sole concern was to make sure that the admiral was safe. Once she knew that, she made a joke of the whole business, and later the same day at a banquet she gave an entertaining recital of the adventure.

Tough she might seem, but her health was not perfect. She lived on her nerves. She had frequent fevers. The doctors favoured the fashionable treatment of blood-letting, the worst remedy for her since if anything she was anaemic. Luckily one of her scholar-courtiers, Saumaise, recommended her to try his French compatriot, Doctor Bourdelot. He charmed her, and soon she was entirely under his influence.

Bourdelot's rivals called him an adventurer. His methods were his own. They were partly psychological, and had sometimes worked remarkable cures where pills and potions had done no good. He sized up the situation. Christina was neurotic and over-worked. He took charge.

'Your Majesty needs diversion! Leave the Classics alone for a time. Give your brain a rest.'

If some men had said that, she would have contradicted them impatiently. But Bourdelot had the French gaiety she so much preferred to the heaviness of the Swedes and Germans who surrounded her. He had studied in Italy, too. He held her spell-bound with his alluring descriptions of the warm South, so irresistible to a Scandinavian. He sang her Italian love-songs, accompanying himself on the guitar, an instrument she adored. 'Doctor's orders' kept away tiresome callers, and anyone of whom Bourdelot disapproved. Even Magnus de la Gardie lost his favoured position. For a year or two Bourdelot monopolized the Queen. Gossip said, falsely, that they were lovers. Only when he had made himself the most unpopular figure in the country, threatened with violence and denounced by the clergy as an agent of the Devil, was she induced to send him away, and even then loaded with favours and rewards. After all, he had cured her. He had made her laugh. And he had talked about Italy.

Already she was growing tired of her crown. She considered abdication, mentioned it to the French ambassador, and even more publicly to the Senate, as early as 1651, when she was not yet twenty-five. She had her inbred distrust of female rulers. She had already arranged for a successor, her cousin, who would continue the royal house of Vasa. So there was no need for her to marry just to provide an heir. 'I would rather die than be married,' she had warned them before. So why not let Charles Gustavus take over his kingdom at once?

The suggestion horrified the Senate. It was hushed up and she was persuaded to carry on.

After her illness and Bourdelot's treatment, she was less willing to resume the more tedious business of a queen.

The gayer side of Palace life went on unchecked. She danced till five in the morning. At one masque she wore a dress that scintillated with diamonds. When she changed it, she had all the diamonds cut off and distributed among her guests. Wealth was important to her. She must have it to pay for these splendid shows and to back her artistic and intellectual schemes. If only one could have enjoyed a queen's revenue without bearing a queen's responsibilities!

From England, at the close of 1653, came a special emissary from Oliver Cromwell, anxious to make a commercial treaty. But the ambassador, Bulstrode Whitelocke, complained that it was hard to get Her Majesty to discuss details. She talked only of the Court entertainments and the fine English horses he gave her.

Christina might have struck a newcomer as empty-headed at such times, but her head was very far from empty. Behind all the frivolity she had two most serious matters on her mind.

One was her religion. She was pledged to uphold the Lutheran faith of her subjects. It had been obvious for years that she did not personally believe in it. Her church-going had been casual and disrespectful. That was known and generally accepted. But it was not known that for some time she had been turning to the Church of Rome. Secret communications had been passing to and fro. It was now mainly a question of *when*, and *how*, so important a personage as a ruling queen should announce her submission to the Pope.

Bound up with this matter was the second: the abdication, which her subjects would not only agree to, but would insist upon, if she became a Catholic. Again she asked herself, when? How? She was thinking of her income. She would have to live in this world, whatever her beliefs about the next, and she could not imagine living in any way other than her present magnificence. She had no intention of arriving in Rome as a penniless pilgrim.

One day she astonished Whitelocke by sharing some of these private thoughts. Drawing her stool close to him, she said: 'I have it in mind to give up the crown of Sweden, and to retire into private life. It would be much more to my taste than the heavy cares and troubles attendant on governing my kingdom.' She asked his advice, swearing him to secrecy, though he might tell Cromwell when he returned to London. They talked for a long time, Whitelocke trying to dissuade her and warning her that she might land herself in money difficulties. 'I can content myself with very little,' said Christina, 'and for servants, with a lackey and a chambermaid.' Brave words! Perhaps there were emotional moments when she believed them.

Needless to say, the ambassador was told nothing of her other secret, her intention to change her religion, which would have met with no enthusiasm in Puritan England.

As the end of the long northern winter drew near in 1654, so did the end of the official life that wearied her. 'When I see these people it's like seeing the Devil!' she cried out against the hapless secretaries who had to trouble her with papers to read and sign.

At such a time of year all Scandinavians yearn for the return of the sun. Christina, however, was dreaming of a stronger sun—in Italy. That was where she would go, once her affairs were arranged, to Italy, home of the arts and sciences that interested her, centre of the Church she was planning to join.

The final scenes of the drama—of the comedy, some would have said—were played out in the ancient city of Uppsala. With its hilltop castle of plastered brick, its royal tombs, its Gothic cathedral, and its university, Uppsala was Sweden's Windsor, Canterbury and Oxford rolled into one.

Here Christina, having made it clear to her councillors that she would not change her mind, bargained with them over the terms of the settlement. She asked for certain lands to be given her as her absolute property. They were not having that, but they were prepared to allow her the rents and revenues for life. On this basis she was granted several Baltic islands, with other land in Pomerania and elsewhere, producing two hundred thousand crowns a year. It is impossible to express this in modern purchasing power. Clearly, though, she would be a very rich woman.

Meanwhile, she was quietly removing her personal possessions (and a good deal more) for transhipment abroad through the southern port of Gothenburg. The thousands of rare books she had collected, the statues, oil paintings, jewellery, medallions, gold and silver plate, furniture, tapestries, were carefully loaded into innumerable wagons and sent rumbling in convoys along the forest-fringed roads. Christina was not too particular about the rightful ownership of these treasures. She considered that family heirlooms and Crown property were hers to do as she liked with, just as much as items she had bought with her own money. When her successor entered his palace at Stockholm he could scarcely find a room fit to sleep in. Even the carpets had gone from the floors.

Before the public announcement of her abdication Christina visited her mother, now settled at Nyköping, south of Stockholm. Charles Gustavus went with her, to be presented formally as the future King. The meeting of mother and daughter was not a success. They were still unable to get close to each other. Marie Eleonora could not understand Christina's motives and Christina could not fully confide in her. They quarrelled at table and the meal ended abruptly. Marie Eleonora wept all night. Christina went to her bedside, but what use were words of comfort now, when all their lives they had been at cross purposes? Christina left at daybreak. They never saw each other again.

Only the formalities remained to be enacted. Early in May the castle hall at Uppsala was hung with tapestries and filled with red-draped benches, while a silver chair was set for the Queen beneath a crimson velvet canopy. The representatives of the nation filed to their places in their various orders, first the peasant leaders, then the burgesses from the towns, then the nobility, and lastly the Archbishop of Uppsala with the principal Lutheran clergy. When the hall was full, Christina entered and walked to her seat.

There was then a hitch in the agreed programme. Oxenstierna was to have opened the proceedings by explaining the Queen's decision to abdicate. But when she beckoned to him to start, he went over to her and whispered. He declared that he could not bring himself to do it. He had sworn an oath to her father to keep her on the throne. He could not break faith with his dead master.

Unruffled, Christina stood up and spoke impromptu for some minutes. She was answered by the Archbishop and the spokesmen for each of the other orders in turn, making long and wordy pleas for her to change her mind. It was the peasant leader at the end who came nearest to touching her. Deeply moved himself, he spoke out in homely phrases: 'Oh, Lord, what are you planning to do? It upsets us, hearing you say you'll leave us all who love you so well. How can you better yourself? You're the Queen of all these countries. If you quit this great kingdom, where will you get another like it?' He went on in that strain for some time. Then he marched up to her, shook her hand, kissed it, and went back to his place, blowing his nose into a filthy handkerchief and wiping the tears from his eyes.

Christina had gone too far to alter her decision. She

now sent for her cousin, rode out to meet him, and led him into Uppsala at her side. On arrival at the castle he was taken to the royal apartments. She had already vacated them.

One ceremony was left. The Act of Abdication must be read to the assembled Senate, the royal power transferred before their eyes. Again the castle hall was prepared, and early one June morning Christina made her last grand entrance, crowned, robed in velvet and ermine, the orb and sceptre in her hands, the sword and the keys carried by her officers. Charles Gustavus stood waiting beside the silver chair.

The solemn parchments were unrolled, the fatal words rang sonorously through the hall. Christina renounced the throne for herself and her descendants—she was quite determined in any case that she would have no descendants—and recognized Charles as her successor.

At this point a high official should have lifted the crown from her head. But, like Oxenstierna, the man could not bring himself to do it. With her usual coolness Christina, having handed over her orb and sceptre, removed the crown herself and slipped the velvet mantle from her shoulders, stepping forward in a simple dress of white taffeta to make her farewell.

That afternoon Charles X received the crown in the cathedral and while the celebrations were in full swing Christina stepped into her coach and started for the south. The summer rain shimmered down, turning the green landscape to grey, but if the heavens were weeping at her departure she was not.

The new King supposed that she would cross the Baltic to Germany. Twelve warships had been detailed to escort her. Christina, however, had done with such formalities. She sent back word that, because of the weather, she had changed her route: she would continue southwards by land and cross the straits into Denmark.

She had, in fact, determined to go forward incognito. At the first opportunity she left her lumbering coach and changed into men's clothes, passing herself off as the son of Count Dohna who, with a handful of other gentlemen, remained her only escort. She made, her old chamberlain cut off her hair. 'Cut it short,' she ordered him. 'Why should I, who have renounced a throne, grieve over the loss of my hair?' So, in breeches and hunting-boots, pistols in her holster and a gun slung over her shoulder, she rode out of her kingdom.

At that date the Danes still held the southernmost part of what is now Sweden, so that the frontier was actually passed before she reached the coast. She crossed the border with an exultant cry:

'At last I am free!'

By this time all Europe had heard of Christina's decision. The ciphered dispatches of ambassadors, the gossip of ships' captains and merchants and other travellers, the blotchily printed columns of the early newsletters, had spread the bare facts and a good deal of misleading guesswork. There were half a dozen theories why the Queen of Sweden was acting in this extraordinary fashion, though, lacking the records now available to the historian, no one then could come near to a true understanding of her complicated personality.

Everyone was curious to see her. The Queen of Denmark dressed up as a maid-servant and waited on Count Dohna's good-looking 'son'. Christina, doubtless warned that there was a second disguised queen in the room, spent the whole meal describing to her companions what a terrible person the Queen of Denmark was. 'Serves her right,' she said blandly afterwards, pretending innocence. 'Listeners never hear good of themselves.' It was not mere mischief. Though they had never met, Christina was avenging wrongs done to her friends.

Once out of Denmark, there was less secrecy about her identity, though she still dressed as a cavalier when travelling (which enabled her to visit a Jesuit college barred to women) and changed into a dress only when staying in a city. At Hamburg she lodged with a Jewish banker, in Antwerp with a merchant and in Brussels at the palace of the Archduke Leopold, who governed the Low Countries for the King of Spain. She entered that city by water, drawn along a canal in the Archduke's splendid State barge, the December dusk rosy with torchlight and bonfires and noisy with the hiss of rockets, the roar of saluting cannon and the clangour of bells. She could still revel in some of the pleasures that went with being a queen.

It was in Brussels, in a private room of the palace, that on Christmas Eve she made her profession of the Catholic faith. But it was still kept secret. The timing of the announcement was important. In that century the religion of royalty affected the politics of Europe. She had so far received none of her promised money from Sweden and she was nervous on that point. She borrowed heavily in Antwerp to keep her going.

Oxenstierna had not lived long after the abdication that had distressed him so much. Soon followed the news that Christina's mother also had died. It was as though all her past life was fading behind her as she prepared to begin a new one in Italy.

It was not until the following September, 1655, that she set out at last for Rome, with a retinue of two hundred people, many of them worthless hangers-on who saw opportunities for themselves in the train of so generous a spender. She rode by way of Germany and Austria. Early in the journey she met the exiled Charles II of England, who had once suggested marrying her. They talked amicably for a couple of hours but it is unlikely that he repeated the proposal. She had turned her back on a kingdom. He was looking forward to his.

At Innsbruck, the ancient imperial city where Alpine heights hung like tapestries at the end of every gabled street, Christina was officially received into the Roman Church, walking to the cathedral in a plain black dress, unadorned save for a cross of five massive diamonds. Afterwards, by way of contrast, she saw an Italian musical comedy and thoroughly enjoyed herself.

A few days later she set out across the Brenner Pass and looked down upon the plains of Italy. Now that her change of religion was publicly known, her journey was a triumphal progress. Banquets, tournaments, fireworks, gun-salutes, torchlight processions, comedies, church services, learned academic orations—the programme was certainly varied as she travelled on through Ferrara, Bologna, Rimini and the other ancient, beautiful cities marking the stages of her road to Rome.

She arrived there in the evening, a few days before Christmas. It was to be a private arrival, with a solemn State entrance to follow later. But as usual Christina's light could not be hid under a bushel. Cardinals, counts and Papal Guards turned the drive into a procession, and the citizens crowded into the Vatican grounds to stare at the royal convert. They saw a plain figure in grey and black. Christina knew the value of dramatic contrast. She laughed to see the throng pressing in excitedly on all sides.

'Is this,' she asked, 'how one enters Rome incognito?'

The new Pope, Alexander VII, invited her to stay in the Vatican, until her new home, the Palazzo Farnese, was ready. He had personally supervised the preparation of her

119

suite, overlooking the Belvedere gardens. A Pope was not allowed to sit at the same table as a woman. That difficulty was overcome by their dining at separate, but touching, tables, Alexander's raised an inch or two to mark the difference.

For Christina those first days were like a child's long birthday party. She feasted her eyes on the art treasures and rare books that filled the Vatican. She roved the gardens, marvelling at the mild mid-winter climate of Rome: back in Sweden, all would be ice and snow, with a red sun peeping over the pine trees for only a few hours a day.

And there were the Pope's presents, to make it really like a birthday! He was giving her a silver coach, a litter and a sedan chair to use for her State entry, with six pure white horses to draw the coach. The great baroque architect, Bernini, had designed these gifts, with exquisitely elaborate decorations, set off by the sky-blue velvet upholstery.

The Pope also gave her a horse to ride, white Neapolitan with Arab blood, spirited and graceful. Christina's eyes sparkled. In a moment she was astride the animal, astounding the Papal party with a skilful exhibition of bareback riding.

The temptation of that superb creature was too much for her. When she made her State entry into Rome a few days later, Bernini saw with disappointment that the silver coach was empty.

Booted and spurred, with a cavalier's plumed hat and breeches of grey and gold, Christina rode her new horse. And as she swung her leg over the saddle, dropped lightly to the ground and strode jingling up the steps of St Peter's, the cardinals assembled to welcome her had to mask any disapproval they might be feeling. Was she not, after all, a queen?

Christina never ceased to feel herself a queen. She never

*Plate V:* Christina of Sweden as a young woman.

*Plate VI:* Maria Theresa: Empress and mother.

got used to being an ex-queen. That was her trouble during the long years that still lay ahead.

More than once she dabbled in politics. She considered a wild scheme to make herself Queen of Naples, using French troops to drive out the Spaniards who held that kingdom. She tried to promote a crusade against the Turks, who had penetrated deep into Europe and threatened even Vienna. When there was an election to fill the vacant throne of Poland she was tempted to let her name go forward, but did not.

A more serious possibility was the recovery of her former kingdom. Unexpectedly, Charles X died in 1660, leaving a little son five years old, which meant another long Regency like that of her own childhood. This was not at all what she had intended. She had renounced her throne so that Sweden could have a king like her own father, able to lead armies in battle. She made an immediate trip to Sweden, and another in 1667, but although the common people gave her a warm welcome—many still thought of her as the 'real' Queen—the men in power made it clear that she had left it far too long to change her mind. Unluckily for Christina, their leader was Magnus de la Gardie, once her favourite but now her resentful enemy.

Christina had one excuse for complaint: her promised income from Sweden was not paid regularly or in full. She was a generous and extravagant woman. She trusted her staff too readily and was often swindled. Her life was harassed by money worries. She pawned jewellery and borrowed from the Pope. At one point she spent a whole year in Hamburg, trying to sort out her financial problems. Texiera the banker helped her. In Rome, where she had removed to another splendid mansion, the Palazzo Riario, her household was reorganized by a new friend, the charming and brilliant young Cardinal Azzolino.

If Christina was capable of loving a man in the fullest sense, she loved Dezio Azzolino. She carried his portrait when she went abroad. They corresponded in a secret code. That did not in itself prove them lovers: a queen and her chamberlain might have many confidential matters to discuss. But the phrasing of the letters that survive does not suggest that they dealt only with staff and household accounts. There could, in any case, have been no question of marriage. Azzolino was a prince of the Church. It looks as though Christina's passion was hotter than his, and lasted longer, but they remained close friends always, and were to die within two months of each other.

In spite of Christina's occasional attempts to return to politics, she was never disappointed in the Italy she had dreamed of. '*I would rather live in Rome on bread and water, with only a maid to look after me,*' she once wrote to Azzolino, '*than possess all the kingdoms and riches in the world.*'

She was not called upon to make so drastic a choice. The Palazzo Riario might not have many maids—she had never been fond of female attendants—but she was surrounded by a host of gentlemen, lackeys, pages and other retainers. The palace was filled with her art treasures. Its windows looked down upon magnificent gardens, with cool avenues and arbours and groves glowing with oranges and lemons as though with lamps. The stables were full of the horses she loved. And her salon was thronged with artists, writers, scholars, scientists, all the kinds of intellectual she had once attracted to Stockholm. Few ladies came. She had no time for women's talk. She froze them out by insisting on strict etiquette, whereas with men she would be free and easy, sometimes shocking them with her language.

For thirty years Christina was one of the sights of Rome, a wonder to be visited and gazed upon by tourists, a never-failing subject for gossip among the citizens. Soon after her sixty-second birthday she became ill, and after two months' illness she died peacefully on the morning of April 19, 1689, with her beloved Azzolino on his knees beside her bed. She was buried in St Peter's, where her monument is still to be seen.


## THE YEARS BETWEEN 1689-1717

Things had not always gone well in Sweden since Christina's abdication, but soon after her death the country had a final flare-up of military glory recalling the greatest triumphs of her father's reign. King Charles XII, grandson of that cousin to whom she had handed over her crown, defeated Denmark and Poland and even tried to conquer Russia. He went far in this impossible task. With eight thousand men he beat Peter the Great's army of sixty thousand, and might have taken Moscow if he had not turned aside to occupy Warsaw. But Peter was by then launched on his mighty task of transforming his semi-barbaric country into a European state, and a few years later, at Poltava in 1709, he evened matters with an equally crushing defeat of the Swedish king. That was the end of Sweden as a great power, and another milestone in Russia's imperial progress.

A few months before Christina's death there was the 'Glorious Revolution' in England, which brought William of Orange and his wife Mary to share the throne of her fugitive father, James II. This was a period of feminine rule in Britain, for, although Mary II was very much a junior partner to William III, they were followed by her younger sister, Anne, who reigned alone from 1702 to 1714. This was also the period of that military genius, the Duke of Marlborough, ancestor of Sir Winston Churchill. His famous victories at Blenheim and elsewhere occurred during the War of the Spanish Succession, fought to decide whether the vacant throne of Spain should go to Louis XIV's grandson Philip or to the Archduke Charles, son of the Holy Roman Emperor—and in due time to be father of Maria Theresa. In this war France faced the Grand Alliance, made up of Britain, Holland, Prussia (just coming to the fore as a fully-fledged kingdom) and the Empire. The war ended with the Peace of Utrecht, and a gigantic carve-up of territories over much of the known world, including the transfer to Britain of Newfoundland and Hudson Bay. French Philip, however, got the Spanish throne, and the Archduke Charles retired reluctantly to his native Vienna, where in 1711 he was crowned Charles VI of the Holy Roman Empire.

Six years later Maria Theresa was born, and not long afterwards (in 1729) the other future empress whose life was to span most of the same period, Catherine the Great of Russia.

# 6. Maria Theresa, the Empress-Queen

The Vienna into which Maria Theresa was born, on May 13, 1717, was not the spacious and splendid Vienna—much less the Vienna of lilting song and whirling waltzes—that later generations were to love. The building of that magnificent capital had only just begun in earnest. The tap of hammers, the shouts of the workmen and the clink of their tools, must have been as much part of her nursery background as the peal of trumpets and the stamping of sentries, for her father was always busy with building extensions to their home, the Hofburg, turning the ancient palace of the Habsburgs into something more worthy of the eighteenth century.

All Vienna, just then, was gripped by a fever for rebuilding. There was a mood of triumph in the air. At last, after centuries, the threat of the Turks was removed. Middle-aged people remembered the terrible siege of 1683, that turning-point in the tide of Turkish invasion which had once washed over all south-eastern Europe. In those days Vienna had not been in the snug centre of Christendom: she had been a frontier-town, peering nervously eastwards into an aggressive Moslem world, for the Ottoman Empire of the Turks included most of modern Hungary and Yugoslavia. But by the time Maria Theresa was born the Turks had been pushed back, not only from the gates of Vienna but from distant cities such as Belgrade. No longer need the Viennese huddle together inside their ancient ramparts, putting up with narrow streets and cramped buildings. The city could expand into the countryside, treat the ramparts merely as promenades. An outbreak of plague gave the citizens another incentive to get rid of old unhealthy buildings and let in the fresh air.

So, rather late in the day, Vienna blossomed forth in baroque architecture, that florid exuberant style of swags and curlicues and cupids which had spread through Italy and the German countries, Spain, Portugal and their respective colonies in America, Africa and Asia, but had never made headway among the Anglo-Saxons, who were content, both in England and in New England, with the more restrained Queen Anne and Georgian designs. Baroque, however, perfectly suited the exultant mood of the Austrians at this date, and it remained appropriate to the splendours of the Maria Theresa epoch. The stucco-covered bricks gave the illusion of a city in shining white stone.

Like Christina of Sweden, Maria Theresa should have been a boy. The Emperor was the last male of his line. He badly needed a Habsburg prince to carry on the dynasty. The other branch of the family, the Spanish Habsburgs, had already died out, causing the War of the Spanish Succession. A son *had* been born to the Empress, a year before Maria Theresa, but he had not lived long. The later children were both girls, Maria Anne and Amalia, who was fated to die before her fifth birthday, and gradually, with reluctance, the Emperor gave up hope of another boy. Maria Theresa grew up knowing that, if no son was born, her father intended her to inherit the Habsburg dominions. Soon enough, no doubt, she learned the high-sounding legal phrase, 'Pragmatic Sanction', given to the decree fixing the succession on his heirs, male or if necessary female.

In time, too, it was explained to her that inheriting the

Habsburg dominions did not mean inheriting the Empire, though her father ruled both.

The Holy Roman Empire, which claimed to have succeeded the ancient Roman Empire, was a loose association of mainly German states. When an emperor died, his successor was voted for by the various princes or 'Electors'. It had become the custom to choose the head of the Habsburg family because he was the most powerful of them. At this date the Habsburg possessions included Austria, Hungary, what is now Czechoslovakia, Silesia (now part of Poland), the Duchy of Milan and other parts of Italy, and the Austrian Netherlands, later to become Belgium.

Germany, however, belonged to the Empire without belonging to the Habsburgs. It was divided into principalities of all sizes, ranging from the tiny and insignificant to the important states of Prussia and Hanover, which was linked with Britain under the same sovereign from the time of George I to the beginning of Victoria's reign. The Emperor had influence with these countless German states and 'free cities', but he no longer wielded the power over them that emperors had once possessed.

It was unlikely that the princes would ever vote the imperial crown to a woman. But if Maria Theresa succeeded merely to the Habsburg inheritance, she would be Archduchess of Austria, Queen of Hungary and Queen of Bohemia. It was a high destiny.

She grew up in the gloomy Hofburg, at one side of the old town. The Emperor had his plans for the palace, but while the architects and builders carried out the work, year after year, the imperial apartments remained in the wing called the Retirada, an old-fashioned, thick-walled place of meanly-proportioned, low-ceilinged rooms and

127

narrow passages. Sentries stood at the doors, the dim light glinting dully on helmet and halberd.

Every day Maria Theresa and her young sisters were taken to visit their parents. Otherwise, like royal children in most periods, they spent their time with nurses, governesses, tutors and servants of all kinds. They had no close friends of their own age: what boy or girl was fit to play with a Habsburg? The natural needs of children, whether for playmates or their parents' company or anything else nowadays considered important, were seldom realized in those times. Children were not studied as children. They were thought of as small-size, unfinished adults. For that reason, once a baby was out of the cradle, there were no special clothes for young people. At six years old Maria Theresa was wearing a miniature version of her mother's clothes. One portrait depicts her in a low-necked gown with a stately but encumbering train. Perhaps, even at six, the poor child had learned to manage it, for from the age of four she had been taking lessons in deportment from an Italian dancing master.

For more bookish subjects she had two Jesuit teachers. She studied religion, ancient history, Latin, French, Italian and Spanish. Yet in German, her mother-tongue, she was never perfect. Though she had an intelligent, lively mind— perhaps rather *because* she had—she yawned over these lessons, which were never designed to stir a child's interest. In later life she recalled bitterly the 'dry-as-dust and boring methods' of her teachers.

Music she learned and liked—the Italian music that then dominated public taste. She played well on the harpsichord. She had an agreeable voice and took part, when she was seven, in one of the musical dramas her father enjoyed so much. There were frequent concerts in the palace theatre.

The Emperor's other great enthusiasm was for riding

out into the forest, three or four times a week, to hunt stags and wild boar, course hares or fly his hawks. It was he who built the Spanish Riding School, adjoining the Hofburg, which with its white Lippiza stallions, trained to ballet standards of perfection, remains one of the most popular attractions to the modern tourist.

Maria Theresa must have been tantalized seeing all these splendid creatures, and watching the daily progress of the immense galleried riding-school with its Corinthian columns. For her, riding lessons were out of the question. Ladies, she was assured, never mounted horses. They used carriages or, in the winter, elaborately decorated sledges.

So the young Archduchess, shut up in the dark palace, stifled by heavy clothes and the strict Habsburg etiquette her father insisted upon, was denied those hours of liberation, those delectable gallops in the open country, that had brightened the girlhood of both Isabella and Christina. In later years she made up for that deprivation. Perhaps as she watched the men riding, a wistful look in the big light-blue eyes, she was already dreaming of the day when she would do as she liked? She was the kind of girl who looked ahead.

She did, of course, enjoy some escape from the Hofburg. In the heat of summer the imperial family moved outside the city to another palace, La Favorita, where there were spacious lawns, a small lake, and facilities for the open-air concerts and other spectacles in which the Emperor delighted —sometimes conducting the orchestra himself.

The Empress had her own hobby, target-shooting with pistols, and Marie Theresa was allowed to join in this amusement. Her mother's chief interest, apart from this, was gambling. She was a rather cold German princess, an ash-blonde beauty, probably deeply unhappy because she could not give her husband the son he so badly wanted, and also because she had had to give up her Lutheran religion when she married him. It was said that she still read Protestant books in secret. There seems to have been no great affection between Maria Theresa and her mother. With her father she had a closer relationship. In public he was stern and silent—he would look infinitely remote as he dined in state in the manner of his time, wearing his massive plumed hat indoors over his long wig—but off-stage, as it were, he could unbend and was not without a sense of humour. He would talk informally enough with the little girls. Maria Theresa he called 'Mutz', the familiar version of 'Maria' used by the nobility.

Apart from the summer months at La Favorita there were occasional journeys to pilgrim-shrines. For her first Communion she was taken to Mariazell in the mountains of Styria, and when she was only six she went all the way to 'golden' Prague, 'the city of a hundred spires', to see her father's long-delayed coronation as King of Bohemia, just one of the family possessions. There she first saw the boy who was one day to be her husband.


Francis was one of the younger guests at the coronation. He was fourteen, very much the big boy compared with Maria Theresa, with lively blue eyes and a tongue that sometimes ran away with him. His worried tutor had to warn him that he really must *not* chatter so much to the Emperor, or even speak until spoken to. But the Emperor seemed not to mind, strict though he usually was on all matters touching his imperial dignity. He wrote in his diary that Francis was '*handsome, well-built, well-mannered*' and that he was '*jolly*', spoke German, and was a '*good shot*'. He even described him as a '*sweet little cavalier*', a misleadingly sentimental phrase (to modern ears) for a sport-loving youth who fenced well, played vigorous tennis of the indoor type then universal, and rode to hounds.

Francis was the son of Leopold, Duke of Lorraine, then a German state but about to come into French possession. There was a family connection, the Emperor and the Duke being cousins. Whatever Maria Theresa thought of Francis that summer in Prague, her father marked him down at once as a possible husband for her. He wrote promptly to the Duke, who was so excited by the idea that he replied suggesting that the boy take up residence at once with the imperial family. This was rather more than the Emperor had bargained for, and he tried to wriggle out of the proposed arrangement, making the somewhat odd excuse that there was no one in Vienna capable of educating Francis. This was in a sense true, for the boy was quite unbookish. His reading, writing and spelling were all atrocious. His father probably felt that, though nobody in Vienna could educate him, nobody anywhere else could do any better, and what was education, compared with the chance of marrying an emperor's daughter? He pressed his suggestion, and the Emperor was so charmed with Francis that he resisted no longer. The boy arrived on Christmas Eve and was installed, with his tutors and servants, in his own suite in the Hofburg.

As the years passed, the Emperor began to have more and more doubts about the scheme. If he was never to have a son to be elected emperor, he wanted a son-in-law worthy to follow him in that office, and Francis, though a delightful youth to take hunting and shooting, was disturbingly dull when it came to the philosophy of law and similar studies important for a ruler to grasp. Also, there were tricky political considerations that had nothing to do with Francis personally. The French were not well-disposed to such a match: they wanted to absorb Lorraine, and a marriage-link between Duchy and Empire would obstruct them. Further, Maria Theresa might be needed for a Spanish prince.

It was she herself who, as time went by, warmed to the notion of marrying her cousin. If her father found Francis 'jolly', it was natural that she should find him an even more welcome addition to the not very lively existence she led at court. What did she care, at her age, about his intellectual shortcomings or the problems of state burdening the Emperor?

When she was twelve, and Francis twenty-one, his father died and he had to go home to take up his dukedom. Not that there was any need for him to stay in Lorraine. In fact, with the Emperor's approval, Francis soon started out on a programme of foreign travel which took him as far as London, but, though the Emperor sent him affectionate letters, he was not given the slightest encouragement to come back to Vienna. Maria Theresa could not correspond with Francis, for etiquette forbade it, but at Christmas, a year later, she was given a miniature portrait of him, and it was reported that she flushed significantly and spent a long time looking at it.

The Emperor considered giving Francis a governorship that would keep him in some remote corner of the Empire. In the end, however, he appointed him Governor of Hungary, which meant that he would be at Pressburg—now Bratislava in Czechoslovakia—a short day's journey from Vienna. On his way there Francis was invited to join the Emperor for some snipe-shooting. He was with the family for Maria Theresa's fifteenth birthday. Later that year, herself stuck in Vienna, she heard with chagrin that her father had asked Francis to go and shoot chamois in the mountains.

Her mother now showed some sympathy. She suggested to the Lorraine representative at court that Francis should visit Vienna on St Charles's Day, which, being the Emperor's 'name day', was suitably celebrated. The Empress said that she would take full responsibility for the invitation and it would be a pleasant surprise for her husband. For Maria Theresa it was not a surprise but a joy which she looked forward to and constantly inquired about. Francis duly arrived. At the gala opera performance Maria Theresa had to sit on the imperial dais with her father and mother and suffer the mortification of seeing Francis in a box with her young sister, but she was old enough now to understand how carefully people of high rank had to act. It was disappointing when Francis came to Vienna again in the New Year and they all went to a masked ball and her father told Francis that he must not escort either Maria Theresa or Maria Anne. Still, it was some consolation that she did not have to watch him with any other girl. The Emperor was determined that nobody should get wrong ideas, either way. The 'jolly' Francis had been warned not to appear with any particular lady at all.

When Maria Theresa attained her eighteenth birthday in 1735 it was clear that something would have to be decided soon. Her education was finished. She was now an intelligent, serious young woman, with an interest in matters of government, opinions and a will of her own. She respected her father but did not always agree with him. She was more and more set on marrying Francis. She talked of him incessantly to her lady-in-waiting. She was said to dream of him continually at night.

Francis for his part, was now twenty-seven and could not be kept dangling as a bachelor for ever. One political objection was about to be removed—King Louis of France was taking over the Duchy of Lorraine anyhow, so he did not care whom Francis married. Indignant and helplessly protesting at the loss of his duchy, Francis was to have

Tuscany in exchange, as soon as the present Grand Duke of that country, the last of the ancient house of Medici, should die.

The Emperor delayed no longer. On January 31, 1736, a little ceremony was staged for which all the main characters had been briefed beforehand. Francis faced the Emperor, the Empress and Maria Theresa. In a formal speech he asked for her hand in marriage. The Emperor replied first, then Francis was allowed to make his proposal direct. The girl turned to her mother, who nodded graciously, and at last she was free to indicate her own willingness.

After the years of waiting she was at least spared a long engagement. The wedding followed thirteen days later, but in that short interval, permitted now to write to him, she sent him five letters, still in existence, which make clear the warmth of her feelings.

The ceremony took place on a bitterly cold February evening. The dark old church adjoined the Hofburg. It was bright on this occasion with the golden flicker of innumerable candles. The bareness of the walls was softened by rich Flemish tapestries, the Emperor's musicians played, and the robes and uniforms and gowns made a warmly coloured setting for the two central figures in their dazzling white and silver. Maria Theresa's dress gleamed with pearls and diamonds, and Francis was by no means outshone in his suit of cloth-of-silver, with a white-plumed hat in the crook of his arm. When they emerged, man and wife, the whole city seemed to rock with the clang of bells and the crash of cannon.

That was all very fine—or would have been, as the last page in a fairy tale.

Real life went rather differently. Despite all the pomp and show, the royal couple were in many ways worse off than a peasant and his bride. They did not know where they were to spend the first years of their married life, and had little say in their own future. Francis was still vainly protesting at being robbed of Lorraine. He was not particularly interested in the slab of Italy that he was being handed in exchange. But he found that even his illustrious father-in-law was helpless. These matters were decided by power, in this case the irresistible pressure of France.

What the Emperor *could* decide, more or less, was the amount of favour he would show Francis within the Empire. Maria Theresa was like any rich man's daughter, wondering how her husband would be fitted into the family business. She could count on nothing for certain. Suppose her mother died, and her father married again, and got the son he had always wanted? That boy would take all the Habsburg lands otherwise intended for her. And the German princes would be sure to vote him the imperial crown, that otherwise might fall to Francis. She saw that her father was not finally committing himself to anything. He would not build up his son-in-law as his successor. He was leaving the door open to a son as yet unborn, unlikely to be born, but impossible to rule out.

For the moment the young couple had a suite in the Hofburg. They were promised an allowance, but there was delay in getting it because, for all the splendour, the Emperor was short of ready money. There was talk of posting them to Brussels, where Francis could serve as Governor of the Austrian Netherlands. No decision was made. Maria Theresa was probably content to stay for the time being in the place she knew, for at the end of the year she realized that she was pregnant. Francis, restless and rather sulky, a reluctant hanger-on at the Viennese court, volunteered for military service against the Turks. He was far away when Maria Theresa had her child. It was a girl.

A month before that event the last of the Medici Grand Dukes died in Florence. Francis now inherited Tuscany, a state slightly more progressive and prosperous than most other parts of Italy, then decaying under their various foreign rulers. He did not rush gleefully to claim his inheritance. He was still angry at losing Lorraine. Nor did Italy much appeal to Maria Theresa. Though she had learned from her father to enjoy Italian music, Florence did not represent to people of her century the wonderful treasure-house of Renaissance art that was to enthrall later visitors. It was, admittedly, gayer than Vienna. The Englishman, Horace Walpole, who stayed there at this period, never forgot his visit. 'The end of the Carnival is frantic, bacchanalian; all the morn one makes parties in masque to the shops and coffee-houses, and all the evening to the operas and balls. *Then I have danced, good Gods! how have I danced!*' But that kind of free-and-easy fun was less available to the new Grand Duchess, hampered by strict Habsburg etiquette, and soon aware that another baby was on the way. Not till this second child was born, a daughter, did Maria Theresa set out with her husband for Italy. They travelled in mid-winter, leaving the children with the Emperor and Empress.

Arrived in Florence, they took up residence in the Pitti Palace and tried to interest themselves in their new home. Francis had a taste for organization and for some time enjoyed exercising his power. Maria Theresa appeared at balls and concerts, and was once prevailed upon to sing in a duet, but she felt ill at ease among the sophisticated Florentines. She missed her children, though the Emperor kept her posted with news of 'the two little angels'. Fortunately, she and Francis remained ardently in love. That made up for a lot.

They did not stay long in Italy. Francis soon tired of

*Plate VII:* Maria Theresa and Francis with some of their children on St Nicholas's Day (December 6). The custom was for children to put out their shoes overnight, which the saint filled with sweetmeats and toys for the deserving or a birch for those who had been bad.

*Plate VIII:* Catherine the Great, by Lampi, 1794.

ducal business and was quite prepared to let others manage Tuscany for him. He hankered after another military command against the Turks, for his last campaign had been a failure and he wanted to wipe out the unpleasant memory. Maria Theresa, however, was expecting a third baby and would have preferred to remain in Florence at least for the time being. She wept at the prospect of going and of Francis exposing himself to the Turkish cannon. It must be admitted, though, that Maria Theresa could weep at will and had a shrewd idea of when to turn on the tears to her own advantage. Francis saw through her. On a later occasion in Vienna, as they left the opera, she praised the *prima donna* as the greatest actress alive, whereupon Francis corrected her good-humouredly, 'Except for you!' So, in Florence, tears availed nothing—and she was not one to stand out against her husband. They returned to Vienna, or rather to the Emperor's hunting lodge at Laxenburg, south of the city, where she was joyfully reunited with her children. Early in the new year, 1740, a third daughter was born. Two months later the eldest caught smallpox and died.

It was a sad time. The war against the Turks was going disastrously. The Emperor refused to give Francis an army to command, which did not improve the family atmosphere. There was cholera in Vienna and the cost of living soared, following a crop failure that affected all central Europe. The citizens rose in riot. Maria Theresa, always ready to take an intelligent interest in the problems of the country that would one day be hers, was frustrated by her father's refusal to discuss or explain anything. She felt shut out. The Viennese aristocrats thought it safe to ignore her (many disliked Francis anyhow) and the ladies were unfriendly. 'So long as the Emperor lived,' she bitterly recalled in after years, 'nobody even looked at me.' She had to pass her days in music-practice, card-playing with her ladies, church-going, and following the hunt in her carriage. It was no life for a vigorous girl of twenty-three.

This state of affairs did not continue for long. In October there was a brief outbreak of festivities for her father's birthday. The gardens of La Favorita were illuminated, the fireworks hissed and blazed across the sky, and once more she took part in a musical drama for his entertainment. A week later, returning ravenous from a day's deer-stalking, the Emperor called for his favourite supper-dish of stewed mushrooms. He ate liberally and was taken ill during the night. He was only fifty-five and his normal health had been strong, so that his death, ten days afterwards, came to everyone as a surprise.

The French writer, Voltaire, commented that a pot of mushrooms had changed the history of Europe. It was soon all too clear that he was right.

Maria Theresa's state of mind can be imagined. There was the shock of losing a father she had loved and admired even though she had disagreed with him. There was the sudden call to take on the whole responsibility of the House of Habsburg, and only the vaguest idea of what it involved or how to cope with it. If she had known that she would have to carry it for the next forty years, she would have been appalled indeed.

She pulled herself together. Within twelve hours of her father's death she faced the councillors in the Knights' Chamber adjoining the chapel of the Hofburg. They were a cluster of old men. There was only one she had full confidence in, the veteran Count Starhemberg, but he was seventy-seven, near the end of his usefulness. Her husband stood beside her, but he had no real part to play in these proceedings. The meeting could—and did—proclaim Maria

Theresa heir to the Habsburg titles: Queen of Hungary, Queen of Bohemia, Archduchess of Austria. But it could not proclaim Francis, or anyone else, as the next emperor, for that required an election by the German princes. So Francis could do no more than stand beside the black-veiled figure of his wife, lending moral support. She was near to tears, but she made her speech without breaking down.

It was not the best moment to have a hundred new problems thrust upon her, for another child was due in four months. She was never one to make a fuss about child-bearing, however, which was fortunate because in all she was to have five sons and eleven daughters. She enjoyed motherhood. She was strong and healthy in general, preferring fresh air to medicines, and inclined to disregard the anxiety of her doctors.

She went conscientiously to work, determined to master her new duties. Her father had told her nothing, given her no training. She felt like a stranger taking over some vast enterprise—and finding it nearly bankrupt and in chaos. She was, she said afterwards, 'at the same time without funds, without soldiers and without guidance'.

The Habsburg inheritance was really a collection of separate countries: Austria, Hungary, Bohemia, Belgium, parts of Italy. They had different laws, languages, cultures, institutions. There was no proper system for running them in a unified manner. They happened to have the same ruler. That was about all. It became one of Maria Theresa's prime objects in life to bring her various peoples closer together and create an organization. She saw all her varied subjects as her children, Austrians, Hungarians, Czechs, Croatians and the rest. It was natural for her to see things in family terms. She genuinely loved her subjects, but, as with the growing brood in the palace nursery, she would stand no nonsense from them. Mother knew best. That was how she approached the task of ruling. As the years passed, she gained in experience and confidence and was less patient of argument and advice. To begin with, though, she was modest and humble.

She did not understand money matters. Francis was clever in that way. It was, alas, about the only way in which he *was* clever. Francis had turned out as his boyhood tutors had foreseen, happy-go-lucky and good-natured, fond of sport and the theatre, given to practical jokes, but disinclined to exert his brain. Still, she must have his help for what it was worth. She persuaded her reluctant councillors to accept him as her co-regent.

She not only did not know how to govern her dominions, she did not know how to plan her own time-table. She meant to learn. She took as her confidential adviser a Portuguese, Count Tarouca, who had a long experience of the way in which her father's government had worked or failed to work. She made him visit her daily, observe everything, and then prepare a frank report 'just as if I were an ordinary person'. Tarouca in due course produced an eminently sensible document, worthy of a modern management consultant, in which he suggested the most economical way to use her time and energy. He provided for meetings and interviews and correspondence, with various time-saving hints, but he left time for her children, recreation and religious observances. She must take her meals and sleep regularly. 'Spoiled coffee may upset the stomach.' She must never let her dinner 'become stale and cold'. At the same time Tarouca realized that emergencies would always arise and that in any case she would not want a monotonous routine. 'Human nature declines to be always the same.'

It would have been easier if Maria Theresa had had

plenty of time to get used to her new life, with nothing more disturbing than the approaching birth of another child. But long before she could settle down to Tarouca's orderly round of business she was plunged into a major crisis.

Frederick the Great (as history was to call him) had inherited the crown of Prussia a few months before the Emperor's death. It was *his* father who had turned Prussia into a kingdom and started the militarist tradition that was to haunt Europe for the next two hundred years. Frederick developed it. He brought in new methods of drill, discipline and army organization that made other European soldiers look like amateurs.

He now sent word to Maria Theresa that he would respect her father's wishes—that she should be recognized as the Habsburg ruler and Francis be chosen emperor—but would naturally expect something in return. He demanded the flourishing duchy of Silesia, one of the most valuable Habsburg dominions. Even before asking, he sent in thirty thousand troops to occupy it.

Maria Theresa knew by this time that she had no army worth calling one. Her few regiments were scattered through her straggling realm, unconnected, each unit a law to itself. Many of her soldiers were deserting because they had not been paid for months. She had nothing—for the moment— to pit against Frederick's giant Potsdam Guard or the solid blue-and-white masses of his infantry of the line. But she was not going to give away an inch of Habsburg land; she held that as a sacred principle and clung to it always as best she could. She defied Frederick, and stiffened her husband's wobbling resolution when he seemed inclined to make a deal with the Prussian. Surely the other kings of Europe would see justice done? Had they not accepted in advance her father's scheme, the Pragmatic Sanction?

There was one great cause for rejoicing. Early in 1741 her fourth child was born, a boy at last, Joseph, the grandson the Emperor had longed for but had not lived to see.

This birth delighted her subjects. She found herself, and even Francis, popular. Until then, the people had been lukewarm, knowing little of her and uneasy at finding a woman ruling them, and having no enthusiasm for her husband. Now that they had given Austria an archduke again, the royal couple met smiling faces everywhere.

Maria Theresa was determined to please more than the Austrians. She was going to charm the other Habsburg peoples. Deliberately she had taken 'Queen of Hungary' as the first of her titles. Now she was going to win over the proud and independent Hungarians. She would go to Pressburg and be crowned their sovereign, omitting none of their ancient ceremonial.

That ceremonial demanded that a new king of Hungary should appear before his subjects on horseback. It did not worry her that she had never learned to ride. As soon as she had recovered from the birth of her son, she started lessons with some of her ladies at a quiet castle near Vienna. She rode astride, in boots and leather breeches, but with a long skirt spread over them. She must have proved an apt pupil, for when the coronation took place towards the end of June she was able to play her part with dignity before the surprised but knowledgeable eyes of the Hungarians. Cloaked and crowned, she had to mount a black stallion, ride up the royal mound, unsheathe a sword and wave it symbolically four times, north, south, east and west.

After that triumphant performance she became a tireless horsewoman and often rode to visit her troops. A woman rider remained for a long time a great novelty, and this custom of hers helped to make her still more popular. She might be a woman, the soldiers argued, but she could ride with the best, she came into their camps, she knew the hardships of army life, and she cared for their welfare. Once again, Maria Theresa's motherly instincts were displayed in her public life.

In those days there were still kings who went into battle with their armies, not only the warlike Prussian Frederick but even George II of England. Maria Theresa did not go to those lengths, however, so that the wars of her reign, though they loom large in history, are only a stormy, smoky background to her personal story. She felt deeply, waiting, hoping, praying, at last receiving the dispatches that brought the news, more often bad than good. But she was not on the battlefields where the grenades flew and the cannon belched their acrid fumes, so this is not the place to chronicle campaigns she knew only at second hand.

Frederick's aggression in Silesia began the War of the Austrian Succession. Charles Albert, the Elector of Bavaria, joined Frederick, and was rewarded by being voted emperor in place of Francis. The French also supported Frederick. Britain sided with Austria. Something like a world war developed, the French and British using the excuse to fight for the possession of India and Canada, or, as the historian Macaulay expressed it, 'in order that Frederick might rob a neighbour whom he had promised to defend' (Maria Theresa), 'black men fought on the coast of Coromandel, and red men scalped each other by the Great Lakes of North America'. The net result, so far as Maria Theresa was concerned, was the Treaty of Aix-la-Chapelle in 1748, leaving Frederick with Silesia and herself with an undying resentment.

Francis, though, was Emperor at last, achieving election after Charles Albert's death in 1745. Maria Theresa took the title of Empress-Queen. In reality, she ran the affairs of the Empire, combined with those of the Habsburg possessions, just as her father had done. Francis wanted only to enjoy life. 'He gladly leaves both the glory and the cares of government to the Empress,' reported the Prussian ambassador. As the years went by, Francis gave Maria Theresa cause for jealousy and sorrow, turning to other women less serious and busy than she was to join him in his amusements. But no public scandal or open quarrel marred their family life, and when Francis died suddenly in his carriage one August evening in Innsbruck in 1765, as he drove back from the opera, she was almost heart-broken.

The unfaithfulness of this light-weight husband was just one of the many things she had to bear, she knew, in a life where she put duty before everything. A year later she was advising her newly married daughter Mimi: 'Try to keep your husband amused or he will seek relaxation elsewhere . . . Wild passion soon fades. A married couple should respect and help each other . . . The more faith you show in your husband, the less you try to meddle, the closer to you he will stay.'

She made a new home for the imperial family in the lovely Palace of Schönbrunn, which still remains, for the visitor to Vienna, the living memorial of the Maria Theresa epoch. She had never liked the Hofburg gloom. Her other childhood home, the sunny Favorita, she could not bear after her father's death. So, at an early opportunity, she put in hand a scheme to enlarge and adapt what had once been a mere hunting-lodge. The result was a palace with a facade over five hundred feet long and a total of fourteen hundred rooms, counting those in the outbuildings. The name was derived from the *schöner brunnen*, the 'beautiful fountain' in the grounds. These grounds she threw open to the citizens from the beginning, so that they could share in her enjoyment, and even in those days the sightseer was able to get meals and drinks in a pavilion which she provided.

It was a spacious, bright palace she created, all cream and gold, window and mirror, but with immense porcelain stoves to keep it warm in winter, placed so that the servants could stoke them from the other side of the wall without coming into the room. For all her cares of state she never lost her feminine delight in furniture and decoration. Her special enthusiasm was for Oriental lacquer, porcelain and wallpaper. Her spirit lingers in the Chinese rooms, where pieces of blue china blossom like fruit on ornate brackets branching from the walls. It haunts, too, the nurseries, so cheerful compared with the dark rooms of her own childhood. The portraits of the children still hang there, and the pieces of embroidery the girls used to work for her birthday. She adored the children and loved to show them off at fancy-dress balls or in musical plays like those in which she had once performed for her father.

Adore them she might, but when they grew up she sacrificed them. The girls had to marry not to please themselves but to suit political needs, to win allies, to cement treaties. The youngest (whose tragic fate she did not live to know) was Marie Antoinette.

Even her eldest son, elected Emperor Joseph II after his father's death, and made co-regent of her own dominions, never broke free from her domination while she lived. He had views of his own, and she had him trained for government, but her own personality was too strong. She could not help herself. She was a supreme matriarch. She must be Empress-Queen to the end.

Her chief minister, Prince von Kaunitz, came to power in 1750, chiefly because he was the only one of her advisers at that time who whole-heartedly approved her views.

After that, he held his place throughout her reign. Outwardly, the two were in complete contrast. Kaunitz was vain and affected, Maria Theresa natural. He was a cynical rationalist, she a devout Catholic. He was obsessed with his own health and could not bear to visit a sick person or think of death. He had an insane dread of fresh air, held a handkerchief over his lips when out of doors, and confined his daily exercise to a precise number of minutes riding under a glass roof. Maria Theresa normally kept her windows wide open on the coolest days: when Kaunitz came to confer with her, he insisted on having them shut. She put up with his fads and mannerisms because she knew he had a first-class brain and was the helper she needed.

For thirty years they worked together. In a dogged attempt to recover Silesia from Frederick, they switched alliances and fought the Seven Years' War (1756–1763), this time helped by France and with Britain on the opposite side, but the result coming out as before: the Prussians stayed in Silesia. After that, Maria Theresa had learned her lesson. She became a keen supporter of peace. She set herself to protect her dominions by alliances and her daughters' marriages. When Frederick agreed with Catherine the Great of Russia to carve up the territory of Poland, she insisted on a slice for Austria. 'She was weeping—and taking—all the time,' scoffed Frederick, alluding to her talent for demolishing opposition by feminine methods. Her share in the Polish partition was not her most creditable action. As always she was putting her country's interests before everything.

In 1779 the danger of war with Prussia arose again. She avoided it by signing the Treaty of Teschen. Now, she told Kaunitz, she had finished her life's journey and could sing a *Te Deum*. Whatever the cost to herself, she had ensured peace for her subjects.

That day was her sixty-second birthday. It was as though she, who had never troubled about her health, had a premonition that her long reign was almost over. She celebrated one more birthday. Then, in the following autumn, she fell ill. She was clearly in pain and nearing her end. 'You are not at ease,' said her son. And with her usual lack of fuss she assured him: 'I am at ease enough to die.' Those were her last words. It was November 28, 1780. The eighteenth

**THE EUROPE OF MARIA THERESA AND CATHERINE.**
Boundaries as in 1748, when they were young. Shaded territory belonged to the Habsburgs, but was not part of the Holy Roman Empire.

century and the old order were dying too. She had lived long enough to hear of the American Revolution, and soon now would come the French upheaval, shaking the Habsburg empire and taking off the foolish pretty head of her child. That grief at least, the tragedy of Marie Antoinette, she was spared.

# 7. Catherine the Great

There were no 'years between' Maria Theresa and Catherine. Their lives overlapped. For a whole generation Europe's two vast empires, the Habsburg and the Russian, were controlled by two forceful but utterly different women.

Catherine was the younger by almost twelve years. She was born on May 2, 1729, in the Pomeranian city of Stettin, now Polish and spelt 'Szczecin'. It stood on the River Oder, sixteen miles south of the Baltic coast, a bleak grey garrison-town in a flat monotonous country.

Catherine was the daughter of Prince Christian Augustus of Anhalt-Zerbst, and she grew up in a castle, but her early life was not nearly so grand as these two facts suggest.

Her father was one of the innumerable German princes who held the rank without any lands or riches to go with it. He had made his career as an officer of the Prussian Army under the father of Frederick the Great. His wife was a well-connected little snob, much younger than he, restless and resentful because she felt she had married beneath her. She was sixteen when she gave birth to Catherine. At that time the Prince was only a regimental commander, and they lived quite frugally in a house with a number, 1, Grosse Domstrasse. Later he was made governor of the city as well, and they were able to move into its castle, a gloomy fortress but more in keeping with the Princess's notions of her own status.

Catherine was christened Sophia Augusta Frederika.

149

The change of name was made long afterwards. In the family she was called Figchen or Fike.

Other children followed, two boys and two girls, but only Fritz survived childhood. The first boy, Wilhelm, was a cripple who died when he was twelve. Fike remembered jealously, many years later, how her mother had loved Wilhelm 'idolatrously', while she herself 'was only endured and was often scolded, harshly and fiercely, not always fairly'.

Her mother she saw several times most days, but she was mainly with her governess and teachers. Her father was a distant figure, because of his public duties, but she loved and respected him. She summed up her parents as she recalled them:

'My father was very economical, my mother by contrast rather extravagant and free with her money. She loved gaiety and the world of fashion to excess: he preferred quiet. She was lively and capricious, he was grave and morally strict. My mother was regarded as cleverer and more intellectual than my father, but he was a man of serious and sterling character with a well-stocked mind. He liked to read, and so did she, but the extent of her knowledge was extremely superficial. Her vivacity and good looks had earned her a great reputation. What was more, she understood the ways of high society better than he did.'

It might have been an unhappy marriage, especially as there was such a difference in ages, but 'apparently they got on splendidly together'. The dullness of that grim garrison-town might have driven the Princess to desperation, but luckily she was able to pay regular visits to her various high-born relatives, taking the children with her, as well as appearing at the Prussian court with her husband when he had to go there.

Fike never forgot those visits. There were the quarrel-

some maiden aunts, living grandly in convents and devoted
to their pets. The Princess Hedwig Sophia Augusta kept
sixteen pugs in her room and 'a large number of parrots . . .
you can imagine the fragrance that prevailed there!'
Another aunt, Sophia Christina, filled her room with birds
of every kind, many of them injured. Fike once opened the
window while her aunt was absent, so that all the birds
able to fly promptly escaped. Nothing was said, but Fike
was never allowed to visit that room again.

There were other experiences on those journeys with her
mother. Once, returning to Stettin in winter-time, they
were lost in a blizzard. Then there was the court visit to
Berlin when she was eleven. Not only did she see the new
King of Prussia, the future Frederick the Great: she stood,
silent but inwardly shattered, listening to her mother
telling a deliberate lie. She had not realized that grown-ups
did such things. If she had spent more time in her mother's
company she might have had this experience long before
she was eleven.

Mostly, however, she lived in a corner of the paved
quadrangle of the grim old Pomeranian castle, separated
by a long passage from her parents' apartments near the
gatehouse. Fike's bedroom adjoined a chapel. Through the
wall she could hear the organ throbbing and thundering,
and from high overhead came the regular clang of bells.
Outside, there were the stamp of sentries, the loud voices,
and the rest of the noise that went with garrison life.

In this corner her constant companion was her governess,
Mademoiselle Elizabeth Cardel, her beloved 'Babet'.
Babet she remembered always as 'a clever girl', who 'knew
everything without having learned anything—she knew all
the comedies and tragedies like her five fingers and was
extremely amusing'. Babet was soaked in the French
playwrights, Molière, Corneille and Racine. She was full

of commonsense, talked well, and had interesting friends, some of them French Protestant immigrants like herself. Young Fike listened to them. In Babet's room she developed a life-long taste for good conversation.

She did not think much of her other teachers. Her dancing master represented 'money thrown away', and so did her music master, for she had no ear, and even Babet could teach her nothing about singing. A French schoolmaster, Monsieur Laurent, was 'an old soft-head' who spoke German 'like a Spanish cow'. As for her principal tutor, Herr Wagner, the army chaplain whom her father appointed to give her a sound religious training, 'I cherish no grudge whatever against him', she recalled, 'but I am certain in my heart of hearts that he was a blockhead'. Poor Pastor Wagner! He was no match for an inquisitive child whose wits had been sharpened by clever Babet and her friends. Fike used to floor him with questions. Was it fair that Marcus Aurelius and other virtuous pagans should be damned when they had had no chance to win salvation? What *was* the 'chaos' that had been before the Creation? What was the meaning of circumcision?

Babet tried to teach her that sometimes in life it was important to please people rather than to argue and disagree. (This was particularly true when Fike dealt with her mother, who was apt to prefer a box on the ear to a rational discussion.) Though frank and direct by natural inclination, Fike learned gradually to guard her tongue and mask her private thoughts. It was a lesson that was often to help her in the days ahead.

Physically, as well as mentally, she was a lively girl, fond of energetic pastimes, and in her early days especially (before they moved from their house in the Grosse Dom-strasse) she loved to play in the streets with the friends she made in the town. But, though her constitution was basically sound, she was unlucky with her health. First she was tormented with eczema and more than once had to have her hair cut off and her head shaved. Then, at seven years old, she had inflammation of the lungs, and developed a malformation of the spine. Her parents, who already had a boy with a hip deformity, were in despair. The doctors then knew little of such conditions, and even less about their treatment. The men who knew most about the human anatomy were the public executioners, whose macabre craft gave them unique experience. So, under conditions of utmost secrecy, the Stettin executioner was smuggled into Fike's bedroom and allowed to examine her crooked back. This man devised a kind of corset which she was forced to wear night and day, most uncomfortably, for the next four years. Whether because of this treatment or in spite of it, she developed into a tall, slender girl with a good posture.

She grew better looking, too, which was as well. 'I am not sure,' she wrote later, 'whether I was really ugly as a child, but I clearly recall that this was frequently said of me, and that therefore I must try to display inner qualities and intelligence.' Until she was fourteen or fifteen she was fully convinced of her own ugliness. Though it is true that she had a long nose and rather pointed chin, she had fine dark blue eyes under a high forehead, and there was a patrician air about her.

Ever since she was seven she had toyed with the dream of marrying some king and wearing a crown. Nor was it just the romantic fantasy of any girl. She had never forgotten a conversation in Babet's room.

Her father's second-in-command, an elderly officer named Bolhagen, used to drop in most afternoons to chat with the French girl and entertain Fike with stories of bygone adventure. One day he unfolded a newspaper and read them

153

the report of a royal wedding. The Princess Augusta of Saxe-Gotha had married Frederick, Prince of Wales.

'Do you realize,' Bolhagen asked the governess, 'that this Princess is not really so well educated as ours—and yet she is now destined to become Queen of England?'

He was wrong there, because Frederick was to die before his father, George II, but at least the Princess Augusta became the mother of the future George III. Bolhagen's general point was sound enough.

'Who knows what ours may yet become?' he continued, and, turning to Fike, who was all ears, he lectured her on the importance of making herself worthy to wear any crown that might come her way.

Fike's mother was thinking about crowns too. She cultivated every useful connection she had—and she was not without such connections, not only in Germany but in Russia. Peter the Great's grandson, Peter Ulrich, would make an ideal husband. He was half German—his father being the Duke of Holstein—and he was only a year older than Fike. Much more important, his aunt, the Empress Elizabeth, had named him as her heir to the throne of Russia.

Fike's mother worked on the scheme for years, aided by the fact that her own brother had been appointed Peter's guardian when the Duke of Holstein died. Fike would have been much duller than she was if she had not soon become aware of her mother's hopes, especially when her portrait was dispatched to Russia.

The situation developed with dramatic suddenness. On New Year's Day, 1744, when they were staying with her uncle at Zerbst, Fike's mother received something more welcome than any of her presents. It was a twelve-page letter from the Grand Marshal who served the boy Duke of Holstein.

'At the express and especial command of Her Imperial Highness I have to inform you, Madame, that the Empress desires Your Highness, in company with the Princess your daughter, to come without loss of time and repair to whatever place the Imperial Court at the moment may be. Your Highness is too shrewd not to understand the true significance of the Empress's impatience . . . At the same time our incomparable Sovereign has expressly charged me to inform Your Highness that His Highness, your husband, shall under no circumstances come with you. Her Majesty has very important reasons for wishing it so . . .'

Thoughtfully the Grand Marshal enclosed a letter of credit for twelve thousand roubles.

For the next few days the guest-rooms at Zerbst vibrated with suppressed excitement and disagreement. The Princess was in the seventh heaven. Fike shared her mother's delight and was only sorry that the business was top secret and that even Babet must not be told. The governess, as a result, was puzzled and hurt, guessing that something special was in the wind. The Prince was gloomy and distressed. If this summons meant marriage—and what else could it mean?—he would lose his daughter to a far-off country, only newly emerged from semi-barbarism by Western standards. She might even have to change her religion, from the Lutheran to the Greek Orthodox, a thought which appalled him, for the Prince (unlike his wife and daughter) took his theology seriously. He was not much comforted when another letter arrived, from his own master, Frederick, the new King of Prussia, highly approving the match. Frederick cared nothing for Fike's happiness. He was busy with his struggle against Maria Theresa and concerned only with winning allies and spreading Prussian influence. Fike's marriage would promote his interests in Russia. The Prince saw his motives, but he could not stand out against his ruthless master.

Preparations for the journey were swift and simple. They must go to Berlin first, to see the King. Nobody must guess that they were going on to Russia. Fike took three dresses, a dozen handkerchiefs, and some underwear. If she was going as a bride, she reflected sadly, she ought to have been taking a bridal chest, with bed-linen and everything, like any other German girl. But she had nothing of that sort, and anyhow she had to pretend that this was only an ordinary visit. She was struggling with tears when she said good-bye to Babet, but she was still forbidden to tell her the truth. They never saw each other again.

Her father went with them to Berlin but the Princess, as usual, was very much in charge. Also as usual, Fike was kept firmly in the background, despite her new importance. Frederick asked to see her. The Princess said she was unwell, repeating the excuse some days later, until the King told her bluntly that he knew it was untrue and invited them to a banquet. Without turning a hair the Princess said that her daughter had nothing suitable to wear. The King then asked his own sister to lend a dress, and so at last Fike found herself at court, seated in a place of honour beside the King, while Mama was relegated to an inferior position at the second table. Frederick laid himself out to charm his young guest, talking (she afterwards recalled) about 'opera, plays, poetry, dancing and I don't know what—a thousand things, anyhow, that one does talk about to interest a fourteen-year-old girl'. The courtiers, amused to watch the formidable soldier and his guest, would have been incredulous if anyone had foretold that Fike, as well as Frederick, would go down in history as 'the Great'.

Now the real journey began, still secret, the Princess

travelling with false papers as 'the Countess Reinbeck'. Fike had to say another tearful farewell, this time to her father, whom the Empress so clearly did not want in Russia, knowing that he was against the marriage. Fike and her father were also never to meet again.

With her mother and what was then regarded as a small party—one lady, one gentleman, and barely a dozen servants—she drove east and north along the post-road to the new Russian capital of St Petersburg, now Leningrad. It was midwinter. There was no snow at first, but icy winds came whining in over the flat shores of the Baltic. They wore woollen masks to keep their faces from becoming numbed. The girl's feet swelled so that she could scarcely hobble into the post-house when they stopped. These stopping-places were uncomfortable and dirty. Frederick had seen to it that they found fresh horses available at every stage, but even the King could not guarantee them decent accommodation.

At Riga things took a happier turn. They were in Russian territory now, pretence could be thrown aside, they were officially welcomed with presents and speeches and even a gun salute from the fortress. There was snow here and they transferred themselves to a long sledge which glided smoothly over road and frozen river. Thankfully, Fike and her mother snuggled down into the luxurious sables provided for them. This was—or was beginning to be—the life!

Fike knew little about the country they had now entered and which was to be her home; and little about the youth her mother meant her to marry.

Russia was already vast, but not so vast as she was to become by the twentieth century. She had been a remote, land-locked area. Peter the Great had fought the Swedes and smashed a way through to the Baltic, and at the marshy river-mouth of the Neva he had founded at colossal cost the city of St Petersburg, his 'window on Europe'. In the south, however, the Turks held the fertile steppes between the Russian territories and the warm-water harbours of the Black Sea. Eastwards, the Russian Empire stretched across Siberia to the Pacific, where the port of Petropavlovsk had been founded only four years earlier, but it would be generations before these undeveloped Asiatic lands would count for much. European Russia was big enough for the eighteenth-century mind to comprehend: Fike and her mother were six weeks altogether on the road.

Peter the Great had taken this sprawling, shaggy, uncouth country by the scruff of its neck and tried to drag it into the world outside—with varying success. Himself widely travelled, inquisitive, dynamic, determined, he had brought in a host of ideas from the West, especially Germany. Some of his reforms had taken root, some had withered, but Russia would never be the same again. Peter had died in 1725, leaving no satisfactory person to carry on his work. In the nineteen years since then, Russia had been ruled by two weak empresses, a boy of ten, and a baby, Ivan VI, only two months old when proclaimed. Recently, after a palace revolution, Peter's daughter Elizabeth had seized the crown to almost everyone's relief, and once more Russia had a sovereign of strong will and independent mind.

Elizabeth was thirty-two, unmarried and apparently without any intention of marrying, though (as Fike was to learn) she indulged in innumerable and scandalous love-affairs. She had already indicated that, when she died, she would pass on the crown to her sister's son, the boy Peter for whom Fike was intended. Whatever the Princess knew about him, she did not divulge to her daughter. Fike would find out soon enough for herself.

There was disappointment when they reached Petersburg.

The Empress and the Grand Duke Peter were in Moscow, another four hundred miles away. But after a few days' rest, during which Fike enjoyed a carnival and the tricks performed by the Empress's fourteen elephants in the court-yard of the Winter Palace, they set off again, eager to reach Moscow in time for Peter's sixteenth birthday towards the end of February. They skimmed down the straight white road between the pine-forests in a convoy of thirty sleighs, each drawn by ten jingling horses. Nearing Moscow on the third afternoon, they halted to prepare themselves for an impressive entry. Fike changed into a close-fitting gown of rose-coloured watered silk with silver trimmings. The Empress was said to be obsessed with clothes, to own ten thousand dresses and five thousand pairs of shoes. Fike must certainly look her best. Even the sleigh-teams were increased to sixteen horses each. The procession went forward again through the gathering twilight. At eight o'clock Fike was being handed down before the brilliantly illuminated Golovin Palace within the encircling walls of the Kremlin citadel. She had reached journey's end at last.

They were conducted to their rooms. Almost immediately a boy ran in impulsively to greet them, and Fike saw her destined husband for the first time.

He was not bad looking, in a delicate way, small for his age, puny really, considering that he was a year older than herself, far more of a child than she had imagined. He chattered away excitably, and, to her relief, he spoke perfect French and German, for he had been born and brought up at Kiel, and like Fike had had French governesses. He knew little more Russian than she did, but whereas she had come to Russia with a brave and sensible determination to master the language and adopt the country as her own, Peter hated everything about it. That first evening his restless, almost feverish, manner could have been put down to the importance of the occasion and his delight in having at last a companion of his own generation. Later she realized that it was his usual condition.

Within a few minutes he had blurted out that he was really in love with a girl named Lopukhina, but was quite prepared to marry Fike 'to please his aunt'. Fike blushed and attempted no answer to this unanswerable remark. She knew that in royal marriages, even more than ordinary ones, the girl must put up with a great deal. As she tersely commented on a later occasion, Peter was 'as tactful as a cannon-shot'.

She could not possibly have got his measure that evening. Indeed, it was a long time before, immature herself and ignorant of many things, she realized the situation into which her mother's ambitions had plunged her.

Today, Peter would be recognized as both mentally and physically handicapped and given special training to develop his limited capacity as far as possible. In a century when psychology was unknown and sympathetic educational methods in their infancy, the unfortunate boy had had everything against him.

He had never known his mother. He was ten when he lost his father, who in any case had neglected him. His education had been in the merciless hands of a Prussian cavalry officer, Brümmer, of whom it was said that he might be fit to break horses but not to train a human being. When Peter could not learn Latin, Russian and the other difficult subjects presented to his dim intelligence, Brümmer thrashed him, deprived him of meals and stood him by the door with a picture of a donkey round his neck. Nature had not provided, in Peter, the best of human material to work on, but Brümmer's methods warped and ruined him. Peter was forced into slyness. Having suffered cruelty

160

himself, he sought a perverted recompense by beating servants and torturing pet animals. His most harmless amusement was to play with toy soldiers, which he continued after he was married.

Fike was spared knowing all this until later. It was ten o'clock and they were summoned by the Empress. They passed through a series of state rooms and corridors, between ranks of bowing, staring courtiers—and there was the Empress Elizabeth, a tall, impressive, handsome young woman in an enormous hoop-skirt of shimmering silver taffeta and gold lace, with a black plume slanting from a coiffure that flashed with diamonds.

They had a warm welcome. The Empress embraced them with emotion. She told everyone to sit down, but since (like her nephew) she was too excited to sit down herself, they all had to remain standing until at last she bade them good night and they were able to get to bed.

It had been a long day, but a wonderful one, and in her innocence Fike had loved all—or nearly all—of it.

No wonder that after all this she fell ill, going down with her old trouble, pneumonia, and nearly dying. The Empress took charge of the nursing, contradicted her mother over the treatment, and finally banished her from the sick-room.

That was the beginning of the end for the Princess. She was out of her class. Her relations with the Empress grew cooler, and with her own daughter less close. The girl remained affectionate but she was becoming more independent, and if she had to be dependent on anyone she knew it would have to be the Empress. Babet had taught her the importance of pleasing the right people. She had learned the lesson well.

At the end of June her conversion to the Greek Orthodox

Church was announced. She was rechristened 'Catherine', her own names being too German for a future Russian Empress. Under that name she began her new life, and was formally betrothed to Peter on the following day.

Life was now a child's dream. She had ladies-in-waiting, money, a miniature court of her own, just as Peter had. She strutted about, giving orders, revelling in her new power—until suddenly the Empress would call her to her senses and she would realize that she *was* no more than a child and must still do as she was told. For relief she turned to noisy infantile games like blind-man's buff, in which her betrothed was delighted to join. They romped as though they were six instead of sixteen. Peter seemed fond of her, as a little boy is, but not with the emotion proper to his age.

The betrothal lasted just over a year. In that time Peter fell seriously ill, first with measles, then with smallpox. When she saw him again, Catherine scarcely knew him. He had shot up like a weed, and was suddenly quite tall, but such good looks as he had possessed were gone for ever. His face was coarsely pitted with the smallpox, his head had been shaved, and he was wearing a grotesque wig. As she was to write in her *Memoirs*: 'He had become quite hideous.'

The marriage took place in St Petersburg on August 21, 1745, a superb occasion in a superb setting, for that city of spreading squares and palaces, bridges and embankments, was already taking shape on the network of waterways and islands where the Neva flows into the Gulf of Finland. The Empress saw to it that nothing was forgotten: processions, banquets, balls, fireworks, bells, cannon thundering and fountains gushing wine. Catherine's father was not forgotten, he was simply not invited. The bride's mother was there, though a shadow of her old dominating self. Catherine belonged to Russia now.

So far as the bridegroom was concerned, the marriage

was no more than another children's game like playing at soldiers. He was still an immature boy with no idea of what real marriage involved. Even Catherine, normal though she was, had an innocence and ignorance impossible to imagine in a sixteen-year-old girl today. For a long time she meekly accepted an arrangement that was called 'marriage' but contained none of the realities of love.

The next sixteen years of her life were to be deeply unhappy, lit only by rare interludes of escapist joy. 'Ten others would have gone insane,' she declared, 'and twenty in my place would have died of melancholy.'

The facts show that she was not exaggerating.

Her mother—whom she loved, despite all her selfishness and snobbish absurdities—was sent home a month after the wedding. She left early one morning, to avoid a painful good-bye scene. Not only did Catherine never see her again, she was not supposed to write to her. Needless to say, the girl found ways to do so in secret.

Her father died suddenly a year later. She was scolded for mourning him. He had not been a king. Six weeks' mourning, the Empress indicated, was quite enough for a father of his humble standing.

The Empress dictated everything. The young couple were told when to reside with her in Petersburg, when to accompany her to Moscow or on one of her pious pilgrimages or on some other tedious and uncomfortable journey, and when to retire to the palace she had allotted them at Oranienbaum, twenty-five miles west of Petersburg on the southern shore of the Gulf of Finland.

She chose their household suite, laid down rules, placed spies to report on their behaviour. If Catherine became too friendly with anyone, high or low, courtier or servant, man or woman, that person was likely to vanish without warning, and be next heard of, if at all, in exile or a dungeon.

As for Peter, Catherine learned that there was nothing to be expected from him. At first she was jealous because he was so indifferent to her and paid flirtatious attentions to other women. Then she realized that these were all as absurd and empty as her own marriage. She hardened her heart. She told herself: 'If you love this man you will be the unhappiest mortal alive, for, being what you are, you will expect your love to be returned.' That was hopeless. Peter might strut and swagger like a man, drink too much, and fill the room with hateful tobacco-smoke, but in essence he was a child who had not grown up. At night he would arrange his toy soldiers across the great double bed. Once, at a sudden knock on their door at midnight, Catherine had to help him hide the toys under the bed-clothes.

She was bored. There was no intelligent conversation in this uncultured society. Just endless card-playing (in which she was driven to join), church-services, expeditions, parties and tiresome fancy-dress balls, when the Empress made all the men appear in hoop skirts and the women in breeches.

She wept often in those first years, but she had too strong a character to despair utterly. She made herself what life she could. At Oranienbaum she had some freedom. She could ride. Sometimes she rode from dawn till dusk. The Empress forbade her to ride astride, so she obtained an English saddle with an adjustable pommel, so that she could please herself when she was not being watched. She loved to go duck-shooting too, rising at three o'clock after the brief luminous 'white night' of the northern midsummer, and with only an old boatman for companion glide far out over the rose-and-oyster-tinted levels of the Gulf. She amused herself clearing derelict ground and making an English garden. Indoors she read, finding in books the intelligent and stimulating friends she lacked in flesh and blood. At first it was chiefly romantic French novels, then it was Voltaire and other authors who, however witty, gave her also more solid matter to think about.

Her relations with the Empress grew worse. Elizabeth did not like Peter either. But she had chosen her nephew as the best available person to follow her on the throne, and she had similarly chosen Catherine as the wife to provide him with a son, to be the next emperor but one. When seven years passed without any sign of a family, she lost patience with both of them.

Elizabeth, whatever her faults, cared passionately for Russia. Not for nothing was she Peter the Great's daughter. She wanted to ensure that the country's government continued strong and stable after her, without dissensions and civil wars over the succession to the throne.

Catherine *must* have a child. If Peter was not the father, that would be a pity, but so long as he was supposed to be the father the peace of the Empire would be secure. Elizabeth herself, for all her pilgrimages to shrines and monasteries, was quite immoral in her private life. She seems to have hinted to Catherine that if she now had a child, any child, no questions would be asked.

Catherine had been brought up in her father's strict morality, but she was no saint, only a normal young woman hungry for real love. Any modern court of law, given the evidence of her first seven years with Peter, would have declared that, whatever words had been pronounced in church, she was not truly married and up to that date never had been. A young woman in that position would be given her freedom (not a divorce but an annulment of the 'marriage') and would be able to seek happiness with some one else. Catherine was denied that escape. She was Grand Duchess of Russia. She must keep up an outward show, pretend for the sake of her adopted country that all was as it should be.

But love she must have, and in 1752, encouraged by the Empress's hints (if she needed encouragement), she yielded to her natural instincts and began the first of her many love-affairs. It was with a gay young courtier, Sergei Saltikov, whose affection for her cooled after a couple of years and who then took a diplomatic post abroad. Most probably he was the father of the boy Catherine bore in 1754, but the child (later the Emperor Paul I) was publicly hailed as Peter's, and historians continue to disagree about the truth, which now can never be known.

Elizabeth had got what she wanted. The new-born child was whisked away to her apartments, Catherine being left, alone and neglected by all, in her bed. A triumphant message was dispatched to Vienna, asking Elizabeth's ally, Maria Theresa, to stand godmother to the boy. For the next few years this far-off godmother was to see about as much of the child as his own mother did, for Paul was taken right out of Catherine's keeping from the start, and she might as well have been in Vienna as in Petersburg for all she saw of him. It was another of the terrible wrongs done to Catherine that helped to make her the woman she became.

She was twenty-five now. Seven years of bondage still lay in front of her. After an interval she plunged into another love-affair, this time with a romantic young Pole, Count Stanislas Poniatovsky, who was acting as secretary to one of her few real friends, the British Ambassador, Sir Charles Hanbury Williams. This was a passionate intrigue in the best story-book style, with midnight meetings and disguises, though Peter knew all about it and did not care. Catherine's legal husband had matured enough by this time to have some sort of love-affair himself with a woman named Elizabeth Vorontsova, but Catherine meant nothing to him. Like a weathercock, he veered from mild good-nature to childish malice, with a good deal of sheer indifference between. Her romance with Poniatovsky lasted a year and a half, after which he returned to Poland: some time later he was elected king of that country, with considerable help from Catherine. Meanwhile, in 1757, Catherine bore a child, Anna, who again was snatched from her care by the Empress as Paul had been. Anna died young, and Catherine scarcely knew her.

How much longer was this state of affairs to go on? The health of the Empress was bad, but she was not an old woman, and there was no telling how many years she would live to dominate them all. Catherine could not help speculating what would happen when the end came. Even the sub-normal Peter had wit enough to dream continually of the crown that would come to him when his aunt died. He would soon stop the war she insisted on waging against Frederick the Great, who was his idol.

Catherine, with her infinitely better brain, went more deeply into the problems of the future. The thought of Peter in charge of an empire was appalling. Even Elizabeth was considering whether the crown could not go straight to Paul—if only she herself could live long enough to educate the boy for his task. For Catherine the issue was simpler: she could be regent for her son, and the younger he was, the longer the real power would remain in her own hands. She had neither the chance nor the need to plot. Peter was hated and despised by the Russian nobility. If it was necessary to set him aside, the job would be done without any help from her.

It was all so agonizingly uncertain: one did not know

whether the Empress would be alive next month, next year or perhaps ten years hence, still dictating to everybody and threatening even her own nephew (as she once did) with imprisonment in the Fortress of St Peter and St Paul. One of her critical illnesses occurred when her armies were sweeping victoriously into Prussia. Her commander promptly pulled back, knowing that if she died, and Peter succeeded, the new emperor would at once show his friendship for Frederick. Elizabeth recovered, however, the hesitant general was court-martialled, and Catherine was accused of plotting with him in the interests of the Prussian enemy. This peril she survived, and some other awkward situations, but she had to use all her cunning and her acting ability, humbling herself before the Empress, even begging to be sent home. That was a characteristic piece of bluff. She had no home now but Russia. And Russia was the country she was more and more determined to direct herself.

She moved cautiously, however—or rather did not move, knowing that a false step would be fatal, and relying on the facts of the situation to produce the desired result.

The Empress died on Christmas Day, 1761. Catherine went piously through the endless mourning procedure required by the ritual of the Russian Church. Peter skipped about gleefully, shocking everyone with his irreverence and his shameless delight that he was now Tsar of All the Russias. Catherine lay low, restraining friends who urged her to act in her own interests. She knew that Peter was his own worst enemy. He would overthrow himself without any help.

Nonetheless, she had some anxious moments. Peter talked now of divorcing her, so that he could instal his own friend, Elizabeth Vorontsova, as Empress. He could quote Catherine's love-affairs, which he had not objected to at the time. And now she was involved again, with a handsome

artillery officer, Gregory Orlov. Yes, if the Emperor wished
to get rid of her, he had a legal case. . . .

Fortunately Peter was busy for the moment with many
other matters. The new power had gone to his weak head
and he was more unbalanced than ever. In six months he
issued enough wild decrees to destroy the Empire.

Bred in Germany, he had always hated the Russian Church.
Now he put out his tongue at the priest celebrating Mass.
He declared that all priests must shave off their beards.
More seriously, he announced that the vast wealth of the
Church would be confiscated and all the clergy turned into
paid government servants.

While setting the Church solidly against him, he was
simultaneously doing the same to the Army. Russia had
been Maria Theresa's ally in the Seven Years' War. Now,
in his hero-worship of the Prussian king, Peter changed
sides, made a treaty of eternal friendship with Frederick,
put one of his own German uncles in supreme command
of the Russian Army, and tried to impose on that army the
new Prussian methods of discipline and a close copy of the
hated Prussian uniform. Still playing at soldiers, Peter
would attend the Changing of the Guard and strike with
his own hands any man he found fault with.

At a banquet to celebrate the treaty with Frederick,
Catherine had to suffer a public humiliation. The company
rose to drink the health of the Imperial Family. Peter,
glaring down the long table, saw that like himself she
remained seated. He sent to ask why. She replied that, as
one of the Imperial Family, she could not stand to drink
a toast to herself. 'Fool!' he shouted. It was a warning signal,
an indication to all that he did not regard her as his Empress.
Her eyes filled with tears, but she controlled herself. She
could not sweep out of the banqueting-hall, however she
was treated.

Fortunately she had many good friends by now, well placed to help her. Even Elizabeth Vorontsova's young sister was wholeheartedly on Catherine's side. And Gregory Orlov had four brothers, all officers, acting as a closely knit team in the revolutionary movement boiling up inside the Army. Apart from mere personal connections, Catherine had made herself popular with the Army and the Church as a whole.

Daily the tension rose. She knew that plots were being hatched against the Emperor. She could not tell what would happen—whether they would succeed or be nipped in the bud, whether Peter would take some new action against her, whether in a month's time she would be a prisoner, a fugitive or a ruler.

At midsummer Peter was at Oranienbaum, surrounded by his favourite German officers, busily preparing an expedition which he proposed to lead in person against Denmark. Catherine was staying alone at Peterhof, another palace on the shores of the Gulf, a few miles nearer the capital. She did not care for its magnificence and was sleeping in a little pavilion, Mon Plaisir, on a terrace overlooking the sea. Here, soon after dawn on June 28, she was roused by Orlov's brother, Alexis.

'Wake up,' he said. 'Everything is ready. The time has arrived to proclaim you Empress.'

She dressed in the black she was still wearing for Elizabeth. With her maid she stepped into the carriage he had waiting, and, taking the reins himself, Orlov drove at top speed towards Petersburg. As they went, he explained that it was now or never. One of his fellow-conspirators had been arrested. If this man was tortured, nobody would be safe.

Not far from the city they were met by Gregory Orlov. They hastened to the barracks of his regiment, where they were welcomed by cheering officers, who knelt and swore allegiance to her on the crucifix held out by their chaplain.

Catherine went from barracks to barracks, winning over one regiment after another. Within an hour or two the troops were marching along the main avenue, the Nevsky Prospekt, in a great demonstration of devotion to her, and she was being welcomed on the cathedral steps by the bishop and clergy. From there she went to the nearby Winter Palace, where her son was, and appeared on the balcony with the seven-year-old boy to acknowledge the delirious roaring of the crowd. There was some understandable vagueness in most minds: were they cheering their new Empress and her son, or their new Emperor Paul I, and his mother, who would be merely his Regent? Catherine's own mind was quite clear on what the position was to be.

When Peter heard the news from his capital, his nerve collapsed. All his life he had played at soldiers. Now, though he had good soldiers of flesh and blood gathered at Oranienbaum, he was utterly incapable of using them. Alexis Orlov marched there, surrounded the place, disarmed the garrison, and took him prisoner. Catherine had written a note asking Peter to sign an act of abdication. He did so without argument, and was taken under guard to one of his country houses at Ropsha.

Things continued to happen quickly. That was June 29. On July 6 Catherine received a letter from Alexis and promptly fainted. When she came round, she exclaimed: 'I am done for! They will never believe that I am innocent!' The letter, kept secret as long as she lived, explained with almost hysterical apologies and pleas for forgiveness that there had been a sudden quarrel at dinner between the deposed Emperor and one of his captors, Prince Bariatinsky. Alexis and the other officers 'were unable to separate them —he was already dead'. It was a vague and distinctly suspicious account. The truth was probably that the wretched Peter had been strangled by the whole group of them except Alexis, who rushed out in horror and played no active part. It is uncertain whether Catherine believed his story and whether (despite her fainting) she had not wanted her husband finally out of the way. At all events, she put a bold face on the matter, ordered a postmortem to satisfy people that the ex-Emperor had not been poisoned, and announced that he had died of an internal haemorrhage.

The ship had reached harbour: at thirty-three Catherine had gained the crown she had dreamed of since she was seven. In time her life was only at halfway mark. She was to wear that crown for another thirty-four years. But her character was set in its mould, the personal perils were mostly behind her, and the main interest now is in seeing what she did with her new power, and how the mature woman went forward along the lines laid down for her by her earlier experiences.

The intellectual curiosity, the interest in art and culture, the delight in witty conversation, all these, first planted in the schoolroom by Babet, were developed in the salons of Moscow and St Petersburg. Her own talk, said someone, was like 'a fountain showering down in sparks'. She was a lively letter-writter, corresponding with authors and scholars and her fellow-sovereigns all over Europe. She wrote plays and memoirs, children's textbooks and an unfinished history of Russia. She edited Russia's first literary review. For a change, she turned her tireless hands to amateur painting and sculpture, to the making of cameos and engravings. Like Christina, she was a collector of art treasures and a patron of professional artists: the Hermitage galleries in Leningrad remain as just one memorial to her work in this field. Like Christina again, Catherine sought to bring elegance to a formerly isolated northern people. She was the first, it has been said, who gave *style* to Russia.

These enthusiasms did not make her neglect her first responsibilities as a ruler. She often got up at five and worked a fifteen-hour day, lighting her own fire so as not to trouble the servants too early. Though she lived in a period when servants were often treated worse than animals, she was extraordinarily considerate towards them. She might be Empress and 'Autocrat' of all the Russias, with power of life and death over millions of people—and a woman who frankly enjoyed flattery and power and glory— yet she could unbend most humanly. Once, wishing suddenly to send a message, she found the four footmen on late duty enjoying a game of cards. With a smiling apology for disturbing them, she took the place of one of them and played his cards until he returned.

A woman of her rank, in her century, could hardly be expected to have democratic ideas, still less to practise them. Catherine sincerely wanted her people to be happy and she believed herself to be in sympathy with the 'enlightened' thinkers of the West, but when action followed such thoughts she did not like the results. When the American colonists declared their independence in 1776, she despised George III for allowing himself to be beaten, and the French Revolution horrified her with its massacre of royalty and aristocrats. She had to govern Russia through its own aristocrats: there seemed at the time no other way, and her one early experiment in representative government (the 1767 Commission which brought together some free peasants, middle-class townsmen and others to confer with noblemen and officials) met with such little enthusiasm that she did not try again. She did not like serfdom. It was akin to slavery. A serf could be sold (and sometimes was) more cheaply than a dog. She hoped that the system would wither away, but she dared not anger the princes and counts by abolishing it. Her throne rested on the aristocracy. No one else mattered in terms of political power. Even the richest merchants were second-class citizens.

Ruling an empire like Russia was, she privately believed, a one-man task. She took advice but she kept things in her own hands. Four secretaries worked at four tables, each with his own sphere of work, each taking instructions straight from her. She was tireless. She drank quantities of fiercely strong coffee and her dress was powdered with the snuff she was continually taking. Good cooking and fine wines meant nothing to her. Her palate was as poor as her ear for music. Despite her demonic energy and her lack of interest in food, she put on weight as the years passed, but she never lost the erect and dignified carriage acquired as a girl in her remedial corset.

Her courage showed in various ways. Plots and rebellions threatened her from time to time. She never flinched. She took a keen personal interest in the security arrangements and the exposure of the guilty, but she forbade torture, tried to see that the innocent did not suffer, and did not inflict unnecessarily severe punishments. Banishment to Siberia was the usual sentence, a penalty that could be much milder than ordinary imprisonment.

One movement that went far beyond the usual scale of conspiracies and disorders was the Pugachev Rebellion of 1773. Pugachev was a Don Cossack who pretended to be the dead Emperor Peter. Thousands of ignorant peasants took arms and joined him. There were savage massacres of the nobility, and once Pugachev came within a hundred and twenty miles of Moscow at the head of fifteen thousand men, but the impetus of his rebellion ebbed away and he reached Moscow only to die on the scaffold in Red Square.

Catherine gave an example of courage in quite another

field when she was trying to convert the Russians to inoculation against smallpox. She met solid opposition. It was true that the treatment had far more drawbacks and dangers than the vaccination method which later took its place, but she knew that these were as nothing compared with the disease itself, which killed thousands and disfigured millions. She underwent the distrusted new-fangled procedure herself and suffered no harm, but she did not manage to break down the people's prejudice. Smallpox continued to rage.

It was not for attempted reforms like this that she earned the title of 'the Great'. It was rather because she continued the policies of Peter the Great to magnify Russia and make her a world power. Even before she gained the throne she had jotted down her dreams of extending the imperial boundaries. During her long reign she realized many of those dreams. She fought the Swedes, the Turks—mainly the Turks—and even the Persians. From the Turks she took Moldavia, part of the Ukraine, and the Crimea, pushing the Russian Empire down to the Black Sea but failing in her schemes to gain Constantinople, now Istanbul. She took the Caucasus. In the north she annexed eastern Lithuania and divided Poland with Frederick the Great and Maria Theresa. The end of her reign was marked by the bloody suppression of a Polish rebellion, one of the worst blots on her record. But to her own subjects she was the patriot Empress who vastly enlarged Russia in Europe.

She worked hard to develop her lands. 'This vast Empire needs peace,' she declared. 'We want population, not devastation. We must make our huge wastes swarm like an ant-heap.' She thought about public health and child-welfare. She sought to expand trade. She revitalized sluggish towns and built new ones.

Once, when she made a journey to the Crimea to view

her new territories, her favourite minister Potemkin arranged for new 'villages' of flat painted wood, like stage scenery, to be erected at intervals along her route. It was in fact just his vivid method (for he had something of the showman's flair) of indicating to her what the country would look like when it had been prosperously developed. The story at once started, and survives in some history books, that this was a courtier's trick to deceive a foolish empress. Catherine was not that sort of fool, nor Potemkin that kind of minister. An eye-witness, the Prince de Ligne, referred to this 'ridiculous report' in a letter to France at the time.

Potemkin had first attracted Catherine's attention just after the revolution which had brought her to the throne. She was reviewing her troops in officer's uniform and suddenly saw that the knot of her sword was missing. Potemkin noticed her embarrassment, rode forward, saluted and offered her his own. He was a striking figure, dark and very tall, with a fine voice. She was not likely to forget him. In any case, he was one of the Orlovs' set, and soon he was brought to the palace to be presented as an amusing young man. He was famous as a mimic. She asked him to perform, and, to the horror of everyone else present, he launched into a brilliant imitation of her own German accent. Catherine exploded into delighted laughter, and they became friends for life.

Some years later they also became lovers, after her long affair with Gregory Orlov was finished. Again, the pattern of Catherine's life had been fixed for her by the unfortunate experiences of her youth. 'If,' she once wrote to Potemkin, 'I had had a husband whom I could have loved, I should have stayed faithful to him all my life. It is my bad luck that my heart cannot be at ease, even for an hour, without love.'

It is said that she secretly married Potemkin: as Empress

she dared not have done so openly. It is certainly true that her love for him was of a deeper quality than she felt for anyone else, and it is most likely that if she had met him in different circumstances, when she was young and uncorrupted, she could really have found lasting happiness. It was too late now. Just as she had no delicate palate for fine cooking, so she had coarsened her moral sensitivity in the closest of personal relationships. Catherine and Potemkin were lovers only for a little while. Then she turned restlessly to younger men, always young men, one after another. She became a byword for immorality. Legend declared that she had had three hundred lovers. Historical records make the total a dozen throughout her life. But those shallow later affairs did not destroy her friendship with Potemkin or their working partnership in the service of the country. When he died in 1791 she cried out in grief: 'Whom can I depend on now?'

As a mother she was no more successful. Paul was seven when she at last gained possession of him. He had been spoilt by Elizabeth and he met his mother almost as a stranger. She tried to make a fresh start with him, but he was not to be won over. He was resentful and became devoted to the memory of the murdered Peter, whose son he rightly or wrongly supposed himself to be.

Catherine, getting nowhere with him, recoiled in turn. As he grew up, she gave him no training or say in the business of government. History was repeating itself in an ominous way. She arranged his marriage; then, when his first wife died childless, she chose him a second bride. When children came, she imitated Elizabeth's heartless example, snatching them away to supervise their up-bringing herself. Just as Elizabeth had once considered leaving the crown to Paul instead of his father, Catherine sometimes toyed with the idea of excluding Paul and making his son Alexander her successor. 'I am crazy about this child!' she declared joyfully. With her little grandchildren she found the purest love she ever knew.

She died suddenly of a stroke on November 6, 1796. Paul became Emperor, a man of forty-two who had never been prepared for his huge responsibilities. The family history continued to unroll like some doom-laden series of ancient Greek tragedies. Paul was murdered five years later, strangled with an officer's scarf as Peter had been, and Alexander, like Catherine on the earlier occasion, gained by his death even if he was not guilty of taking part in it. So, for another century it continued, with more assassinations, plots and revolutions, until the murder of the last Emperor and his family in 1918, when the old imperial Russia that Catherine had done so much to create went down in utter and final ruin.

## SUGGESTIONS FOR FURTHER READING

Most of the queens in this book are dealt with very fully in numerous detailed biographies and other studies, and readers may need to make the final choice themselves, according to their needs, for some books are scholarly, some entertaining and some fortunately manage to be both. The following short list may help to begin with.

*Cleopatra, the Story of A Queen*, by Emil Ludwig, 1937. *Life and Times of Cleopatra*, by Sir Arthur Weigall, 1924.

*The Rebellion of Boudicca*, by Donald R. Dudley and Graham Webster, 1962. (Containing all the known facts.)

*The End of the Roman World*, by Stewart Perowne, 1966. *Decline and Fall of the Roman Empire*, by Edward Gibbon. (There is no full biography of Galla Placidia.)

*The Castles and the Crown*, by Townsend Miller, 1963. (Admirable book on Isabella and her family, with its own very full list of other titles.)

*Life of Christina of Sweden*, by Alfred Neumann, 1935. *The Sibyl of the North*, by Faith Compton Mackenzie, 1934.

*Maria Theresa*, by J. F. Bright, 1910. *Empress Maria Theresa*, by R. Pick, 1966.

*Catherine the Great*, by E. M. Almedingen, 1963. *Catherine the Great*, by Katharine Anthony, 1926. *Catherine the Great*, by Zoé Oldenbourg, 1965.

# ACKNOWLEDGEMENTS

The publishers and author wish to thank the following for permission to reproduce photographs:

*Radio Times Hulton Picture Library:* Plates Ia, V and VI

*The British Museum:* Plates Ib, Ic and IIa

*The Mansell Collection:* Plates IIb, IV and VIII

*Fotofast, Bologna:* Plate IIIb

*Kunsthistorischen Museum, Wien:* Plate VII